LOOKING WITHIN

Indian Art Series

LOOKING WITHIN

Shobha Broota

MOSA
MUSEUM OF SACRED ART

NIYOGI BOOKS

MOSA
MUSEUM OF SACRED ART

Director
Martin Gurvich
Curator
Sushma K. Bahl
General Manager
Raymond Hoogenboom
Collections
Anushka Hoogenboom
Publishing
Phelelani Mdabe
Website
Dario Knez

Belgium
General Manager
Raymond Hoogenboom
Reception
Maria Grison • Patience Offei • Bergita Gjergjaj
Château de Petite Somme, B-6940, Septon (Durbuy), Belgium
t: +32 (0)86 43 30 22 • *e*: info@mosabelgium.com • www.mosabelgium.com

Italy
General Manager
Patrizio Landolfi
Via Scopeti 106/108, San Casciano in Val di Pesa, 50026, Florence, Italy
t: +39 (055) 82 00 54 • *e*: info@mosaitaly.com • www.mosaitaly.com

Catalog
Texts
Sushma K. Bahl • Shobha Broota • Keshav Malik
Designer
Phelelani Mdabe
Photography
Shobha Broota

ISBN: 978-93-83098-46-0

Marketed world wide by
NIYOGI BOOKS
D-78, Okhla Industrial Area, Phase-I, New Delhi-110 020, INDIA
Tel: 91-11-26816301, 49327000, Fax: 91-11-26810483, 26813830
Email: niyogibooks@gmail.com, Website: www.niyogibooksindia.com

CONTENTS

7
Foreword
H.E. M.S. Puri
Ambassador of India in Belgium

9
Preface
Martin Gurvich

11
Soul Search
Sushma K. Bahl

14
Words from the Artist
Shobha Broota

16
Works

52
Shobha Brootha Bio

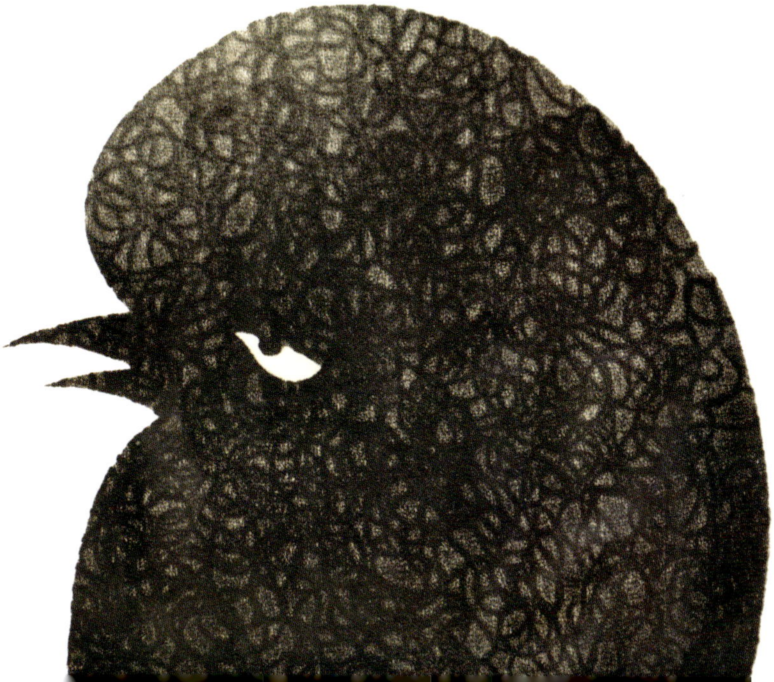

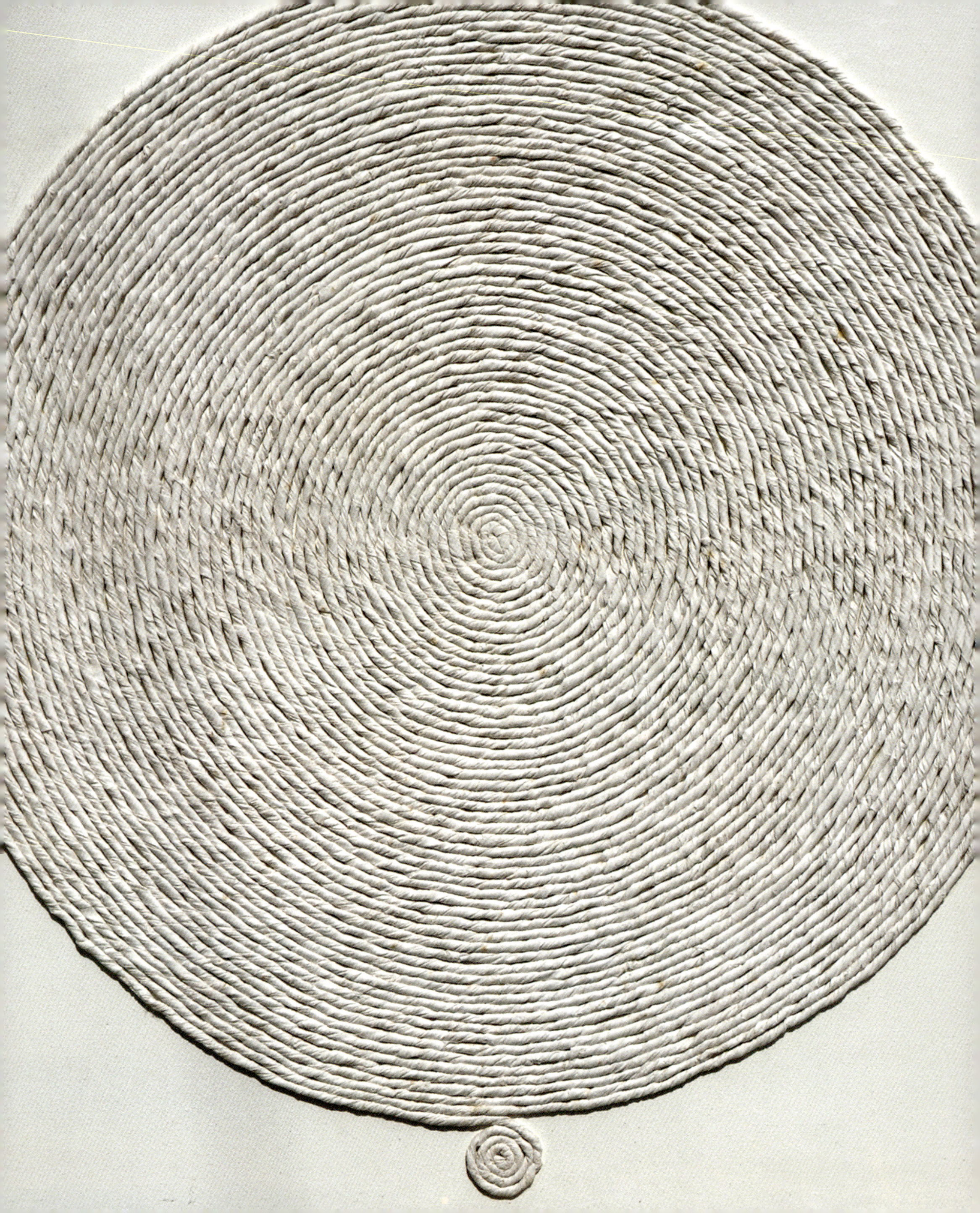

FOREWORD

Ambassador

भारतीय राजदूतावास

EMBASSY OF INDIA

CHAUSSEE DE VLEURGAT, 217
1050, BRUXELLES
TEL. 640 91 40
FAX 648 96 38

सत्यमेव जयते

March 10, 2014

MESSAGE

"I am delighted that the prestigious Museum of Sacred Art is organizing exhibitions of three prominent Indian artists in Belgium aimed at amalgamating different forms of spirituality associated with diverse global faiths through fine arts.

The theme of the exhibitions—Forms of Devotion—is apt in the context of the expositions that celebrate the multiplicity, diversity, creativity and vibrancy of devotional art of India in varied hues and forms. The unique paintings and calligraphic works of the Indian artists--Posapati Parameshwar Raju, Raghupati Bhat and Shobha Broota—transcend faiths and genres—figurative, mythological, abstract, Hindu, Muslim, Christian, Sikh, Buddhist, Jain etc – and showcase the dynamic multi-religious and multi-cultural life of India to the west.

The antiquity of Indian civilization matched by the vastness of its geographical extent has contributed to the rich and multiple art forms of India. These art forms have been successfully presented by the Museum of Sacred Art not only in Belgium, but also in the whole of Europe over the last five years since its inception. I deeply appreciate the initiative of the Museum to encourage interfaith dialogue through fine arts as manifested in these upcoming exhibitions.

I am confident that the Indian art- loving people of Europe would once again have the opportunity to witness Indian mythology, icons and folk tales through the forthcoming exhibitions and that too after the just concluded Europalia-India Festival.

I convey my best wishes to the Museum of Sacred Art of Belgium for a successful organization of the forthcoming exhibitions".

(M.S. Puri)

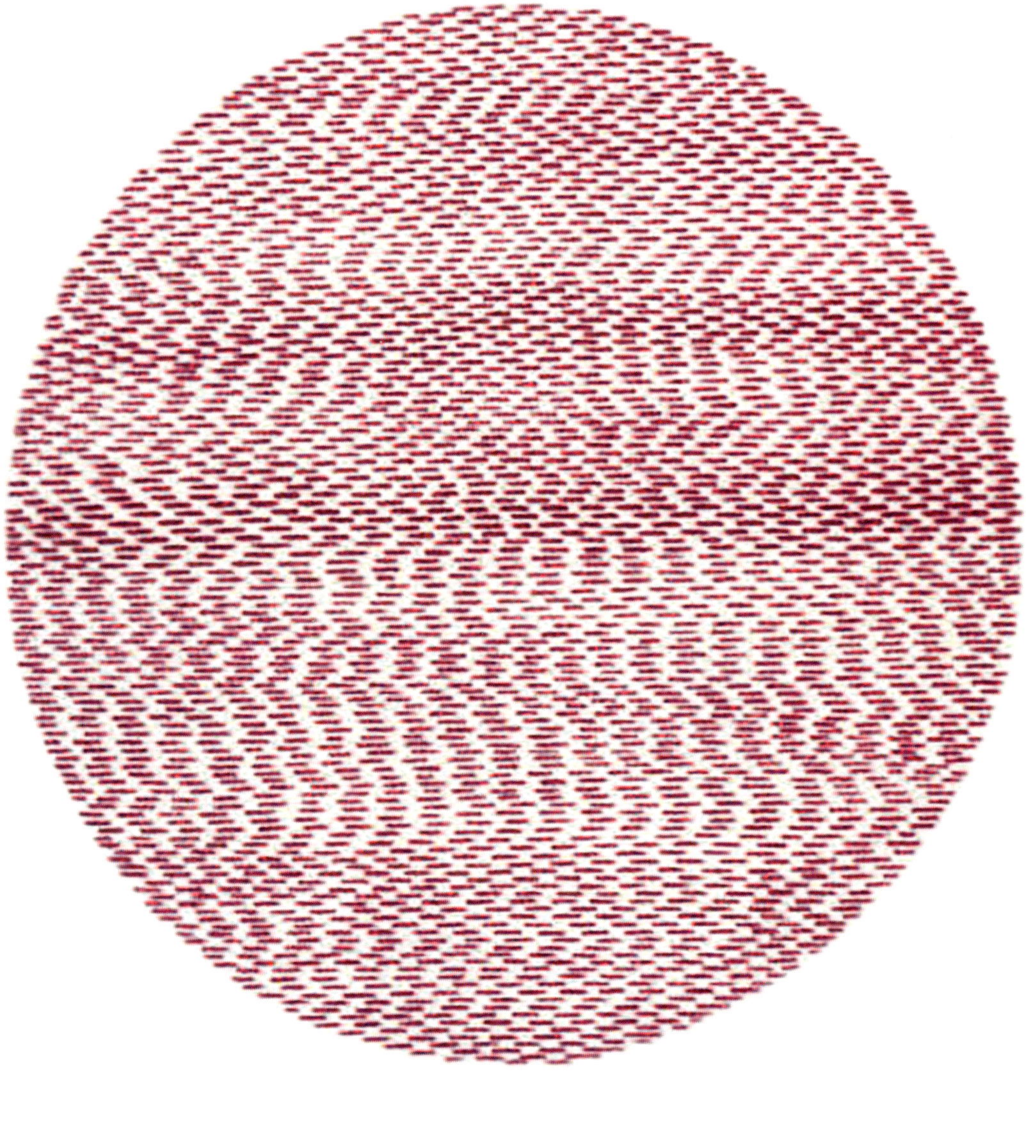

PREFACE

The prospect of inaugurating the 2014 art exhibits at MOSA with such outstanding, accomplished artists as Shobha Broota, Raghupati Bhat, and Poosapati Parameshwar Raju fills me with profound joy.

The inauguration will be attended by our guest of honor His Excellency M.S. Puri, ambassador of India to Belgium and the EU, and art curator Sushma K. Bahl, who has written the texts about all three artists. Moreover, this festive event will be graced by musical performances by celebrated flautist Panditji Hariprasad Chaurasia and renowned sitar player Subrata De.

Our exhibition program for Indian and International artists working on spiritual, devotional and sacred art is quite dynamic and our galleries in Belgium (Radhadesh, Durbuy) and Italy (Villa Vrindavan, Florence) will be showcasing many of them in the upcoming years.

MOSA's goal is to bridge the cultural divide between India and Europe and between material and spiritual life. Art is a perfect medium to do so, and we hope that many Europeans will discover the excellent Indian artists who try to convey a spiritual message.

We are convinced that MOSA's visitors will come to appreciate and enjoy the currently exhibited work of all three artists. Shobha Broota, a senior and widely-exhibited artist, has kindly and enthusiastically agreed to exhibit her art at MOSA. We value meditation and devotion as part of every individual's quest for spirituality and therefore laud Shobha's spiritual approach to the visual arts. Her work is an important addition to the more devotional exhibits in our galleries, and we want to share her art with our visitors, who, I am sure, will enter a meditative mood upon seeing it, for Shobha's works remind us of our eternal and steady nature as spirit souls. In contrast with the turbulent and temporary nature of material life, Shobha's beautiful and pacifying works bring us closer to our real, eternal nature and put us on the path of spiritual realization where genuine feelings of devotion can manifest in our hearts.

We are also honored and delighted that Shobha Broota has agreed to be present at the opening of MOSA's 2014 art exhibits, and we hope that her works will leave a lasting impression on all MOSA visitors. May MOSA serve as an instrument in uplifting its visitor's consciousness through the visual arts, and may there be many artists who will share their art with future audiences visiting Radhadesh.

Martin Gurvich
Director

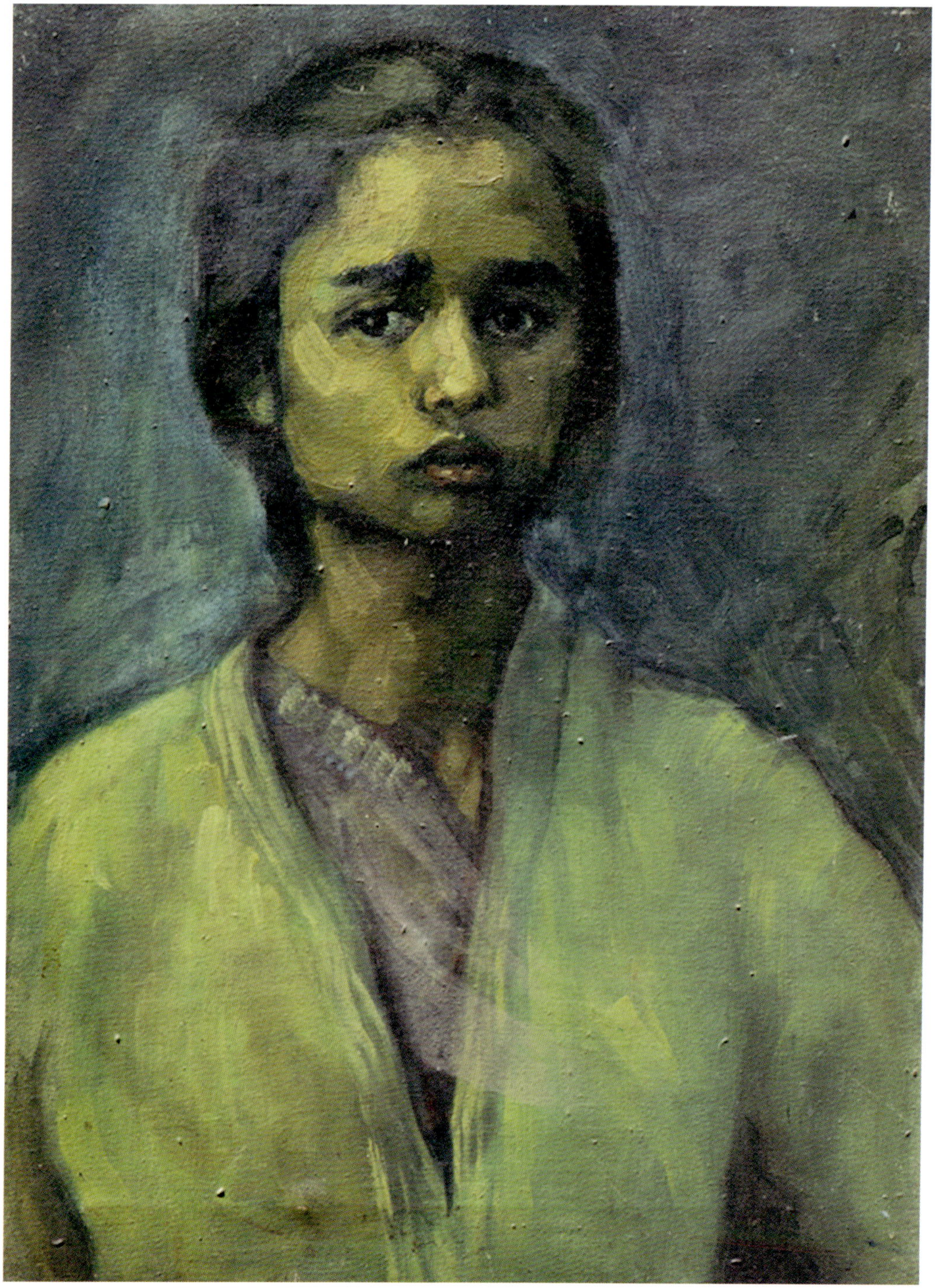

'Self potrait' – Shobha Broota

SOUL SEARCH

Sushma K. Bahl

"My work is a journey in search of my own self" declares Shobha Broota. Sitting in her studio with calm and poise, she exudes the confidence of a multi-talented artist at peace with herself. Hers has been a meditative cruise through the arts over five decades. From mindfulness to shunya (nothingness), in a realm of eternity, hers has been an intuitive and spontaneous exploration of the self within, a search for inner tranquility and quiet – in essence a soul search. Traversing through space, entailing color and expanse, her art flows in simple yet subtle etchings, as they move through the mystical world of silent visual communication. Her work's freedom within an engagingly minimalist oeuvre that sheds all superfluous trappings involves a surrender that endows her work with its distinct harmony.

Shobha's meditative soul search through art seems natural, given her upbringing in a family of artists ingrained in devotional tradition. Like her persona, from musician to artist cum art teacher, her creative sojourn has also undergone changes.

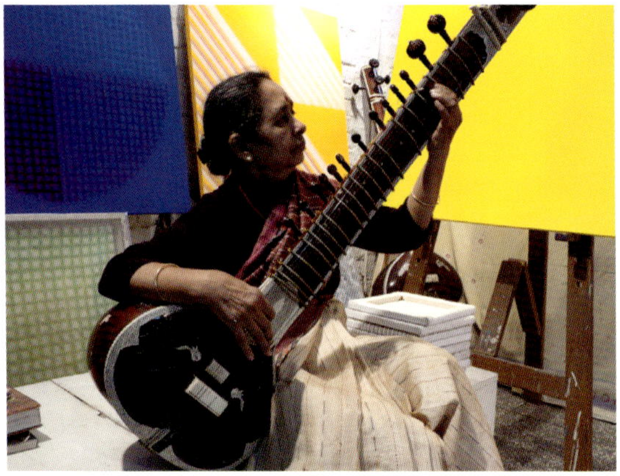

Her earlier repertoire's portraits and human forms, birds and animals, and similar elements have now given way to the cosmic world and natural elements pulsating with organic energy – water, air and space. Her training as a musician, as well as her experience as an artist and art teacher, have impacted her work, wherein aesthetics and the tactile quality of the composition assume prime importance. Spontaneity, without any pre-conceived ideas or prepared background, intertwined with a meditative stance, mark

Sushma K. Bahl MBE is an independent arts adviser, writer, and curator of cultural projects, based in Delhi. She is the author of 5000 Years of Indian Art, and former head of the Arts and Culture, British Council, India. Amongst other projects Bahl was the guest director for XI Triennale-India 2005, the project consultant for Bharat Rang Mahotsav X11, and jury member for the 14th Asian Art Biennale Bangladesh 2010,and the curator of India-ASEAN artists' residency and exhibition in 2012. Ways of Seeing won her the best-curated group show IHC Art India Award. Bahl is both editor and contributor for catalogs and artists' books, including those on Thota Vaikuntam, Paresh Maity, Satish Gupta, Sarla Chandra, and Shuvaprasanna. She is also a trustee and advisory board member of cultural institutions both in India and abroad.

this artist's simplistic imagery. Starting at the center, perceived as the inner eye and place of refuge, she works on the periphery to evoke the soul and spirit. Applying paint in layers – practically flicking it on with a brush but without touching the canvas – her pain-staking and minute work creates repetitive patterns resulting in organic, almost molecular formations. Simple lines and shapes, concentric circles and spirals, triangles and squares wherein light and movement emanate from the center, are re-presented as numerous abstract expressions. The spirit of both tantric and Zen pervades her simple minimalist work with its optical illusion of points and counter-points in repetitive patterns.

With discipline and perseverance, the artist paints layer-by-layer, merging and submerging tones, as indefinable structures begin to make formations. A cosmic play of ideas, such as birth and death, or visions that include light and darkness, and the continuum and vagaries of nature, seem to underline much of the work. Moreover, her colors are symbolic of the different realms and the five senses that human beings are endowed with. The blue of the sky and seas represents the rhythm of the cosmic world.

The red and orange bring alive the art-work's passion and mystique. The yellow pulsates and vibrates with life. Green resonates continuity and nature. And white evokes peace and harmony. Meditating and com-municating with her soul while painting and listening to or practicing classical music, often leaves the artist no room or need to use any words or even titles in her work. Patterns within abstraction alongside suggestions of geometric designs appear as hallmarks of Shobha's aesthetics.

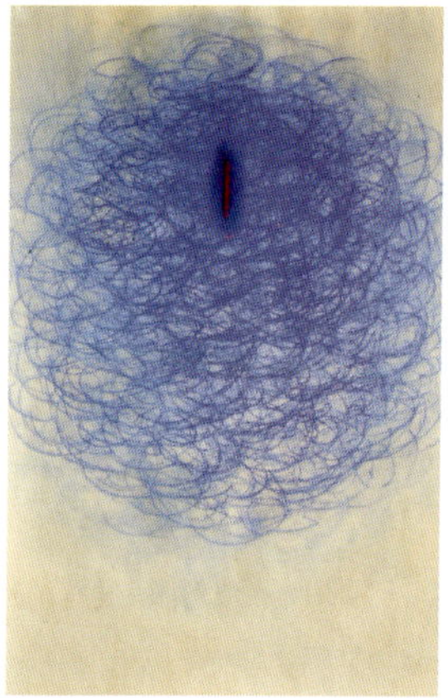

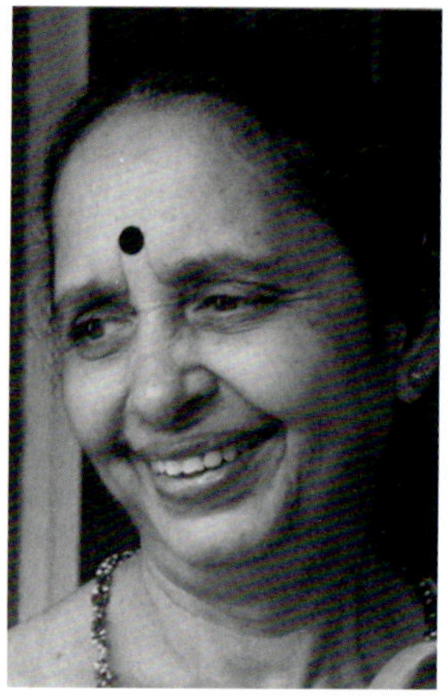

The artist works on canvas, board, and paper, at times large and at other times small. She paints in acrylic and with pastels, draws with pen and ink, and amongst other mediums, works with thread, wool, cloth, wire mesh, and thermocol balls. For her work with wool, she takes time to knit patterns and designs before applying them to the canvas. The collection includes paintings and other compositions featuring small square panels and large canvases in shapes varying from circles to rectangles and lines. There is an abundance of spirals and concentric circles that contract and expand in numerous ways to create an optical illusion of hard and soft lines and forms in a subtle and soft palette within her essentially minimalist abstract oeuvre. A flicker here and a mystery there, a dot in the center or a line in the corner, suffice to complete the composi-tion, leaving no scope for any further render-ings or wanderings. Ethereal and soulful, the work suggests varied shades and hues of the five elements of nature and the seven colors of the rainbow. Her art reverberates with the echoes of the fluctuations between void and solitude, movement and music. It is symbolic of timelessness, a bridge between mind and matter.

The present collection encompasses almost the entire range of mediums that the artist works in. It features a series of dry pastels on paper, as well as acrylic and oil paintings on canvas. There are also creations using knitted and patterned wool and thread that entail the pieces' entire surface. The smaller works are as engaging as the larger compositions. The display includes varied forms and symbols. There are circles and semicircles suggestive of the cosmic dance and the sun and the moon. Squares within a circle in some, and a cobweb-like pattern in others, add another dimension to the imagery. The faint lines and markings evoke an impressionist abstract oeuvre. Her palette is subtle and varied. The spread is rich in color and soft in shade and tint. There are works bathed in reds, yellows and oranges, while others are suffused in blues, greens, browns, mauves, and pinks. There is a perfect harmony of forms and palette in her compositions.

Shobha's nuanced abstractions generate impressions of designed imagery and are featured in the biennials and triennials at Havana, Delhi, Dhaka, and Ankara, and are not only part of the collections at the National Gallery of Modern Art in Delhi but also at Kuala Lampur, alongside the collections of E.M. School and Chester Herwitz, amongst many others. Suggestive of sacred holistic architectural forms, her artistic catharsis helps clear the excess energies of the mind and bring calm to the restless soul.

Because the artist is comfortable in her own skin and genre, her ethereal work reverberates with eternal ideas open to inner space leading the way of the soul search.

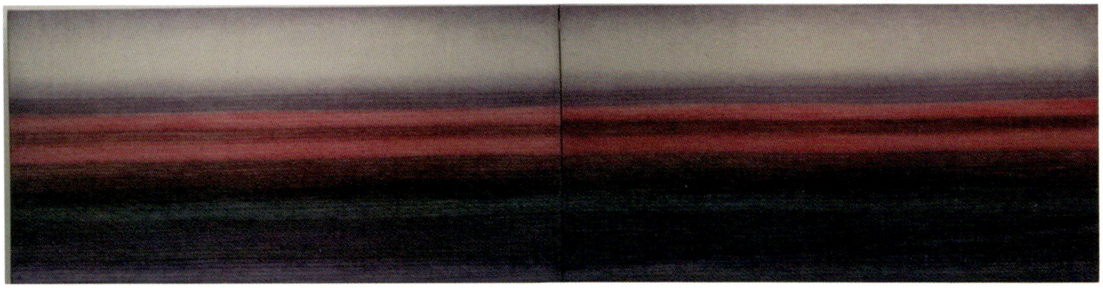

WORDS FROM THE ARTIST

Shobha Broota

We are all born… and then we go through conditioning. We are taught to live in a certain way. Slowly we get bound by the beautiful frills of life. We live blindly, thinking this is it. But somewhere deep down, I knew this is not the true life. It is all made up of conveniences. Once I realized this, I surrendered. I found there is another realm of existence from where life is being guided. In surrender, there is no longer any fight and struggle within, but life simply flows…

Being an artist is and has been a truly liberating experience. Much is achieved when I live in silence. My work is a journey in search of my own self. It is the experience of space, color, expanse and movement through which I travel into this mystical world. My work is geared towards a silent inner communication.

My journey as an artist has been a progression from detailed realism to "Essence-ial-ism." For me, creativity is an exploration within my inner being, where intuitiveness and spontaneity take me beyond the limits of my "thinking-mind" into "no-mind." I aspire to find peace, quiet and harmony through my work.

All creations are born from Nothingness and lead into Nothingness. The process of creation gives me joy and insight into the realm of eternity. I feel blessed being a participant in this eternal drama of knowing this Nothingness. My desire to translate my intense experiences of life to the empty space of a canvas is the driving force. I aspire to feel the limitlessness of the immaterial through the limits of the material. The process of painting itself inspires and rejuvenates me.

I enjoy the visual phenomenon of nature, the cosmic play of birth and growth, darkness and the patterns and repetitions created by nature. My intrinsic relationship with music takes me deep into the world of resonance, abstraction and meditation, which is reflected in my work. I am a witness to the Source from where all of my creative expression flows. It is a continuous movement that shapes my various creations. It seems there is no beginning and no end to this flow. Each work is just a fraction of the continuity of this movement.

I do not preconceive or prepare for the purpose of painting. Sitting in silence before a blank canvas, I contemplate. Intuitively, I start applying pigment layer by layer, merging one tone with another, one color with another. I play with the structural formation, and suddenly I realize that there is nothing more to it. The work completes itself. Just a flicker can reveal mysteries. One dot, one line says so much to me that the message gets disturbed if I try to expand or do something more to it. Sometimes just the color makes me plunge deeper. Just by sitting in front of a color, I can wander to different realms. It becomes an end in itself. Whenever I go wrong in my work, I take it as a blessing.

It motivates me to change and create something new. Painting gives me total freedom, but this freedom implies a lot of discipline, poise, focus, clarity and perseverance. I have used the experience of contraction and expansion in numerous ways in my work and life.

I try my best to shed away all that is unnecessary and come to the minimum in expression. I have realized that the truth of simplicity and the use of the minimum is enough to achieve the maximum. And this is my essence.

Complete devotion and surrender is required for my kind of work. This surrender is my guiding force. It becomes easy to create, and the work moves harmoniously, as "I am not the doer." This method of work leaves me happy. In exploration I do not know what I will find, and thus it is always a revelation.

Starting work from the centre and moving towards the periphery is an unending process. I feel the centre is the place of refuge for peace and quiet. It takes me within, and that is where I would like to rest.

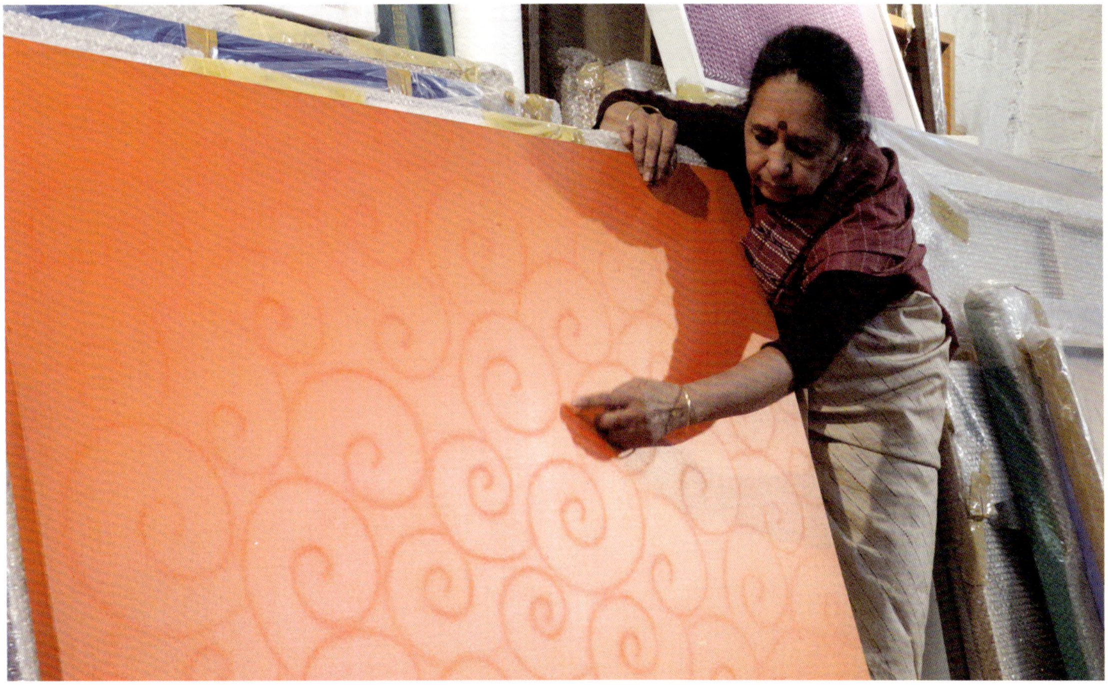

Over here, the cosmic forms of, let us say, is a sacral geometry. The target, pin-pointed order, is compelling. The blue eye at the very centre portends profundity, carries, to the viewer the rigour of full conviction. The image may be deemed a steady, emphatic icon.

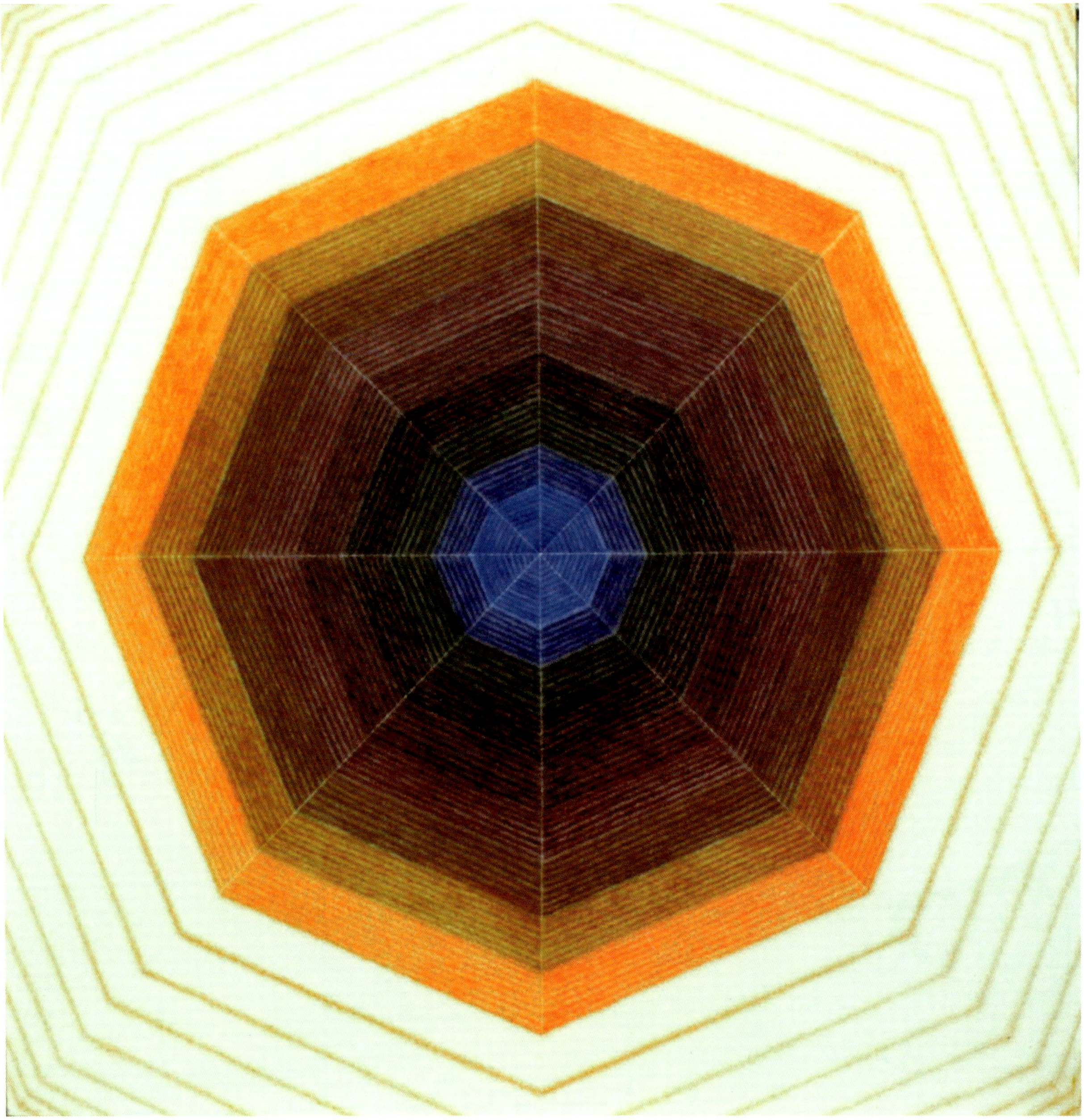

Untitled
Acrylic & oil on canvas, 122 x 122 cm

Origin
Dry pastels on paper, 25 x 25 cm

Origin
Dry pastels on paper, 25 x 25 cm

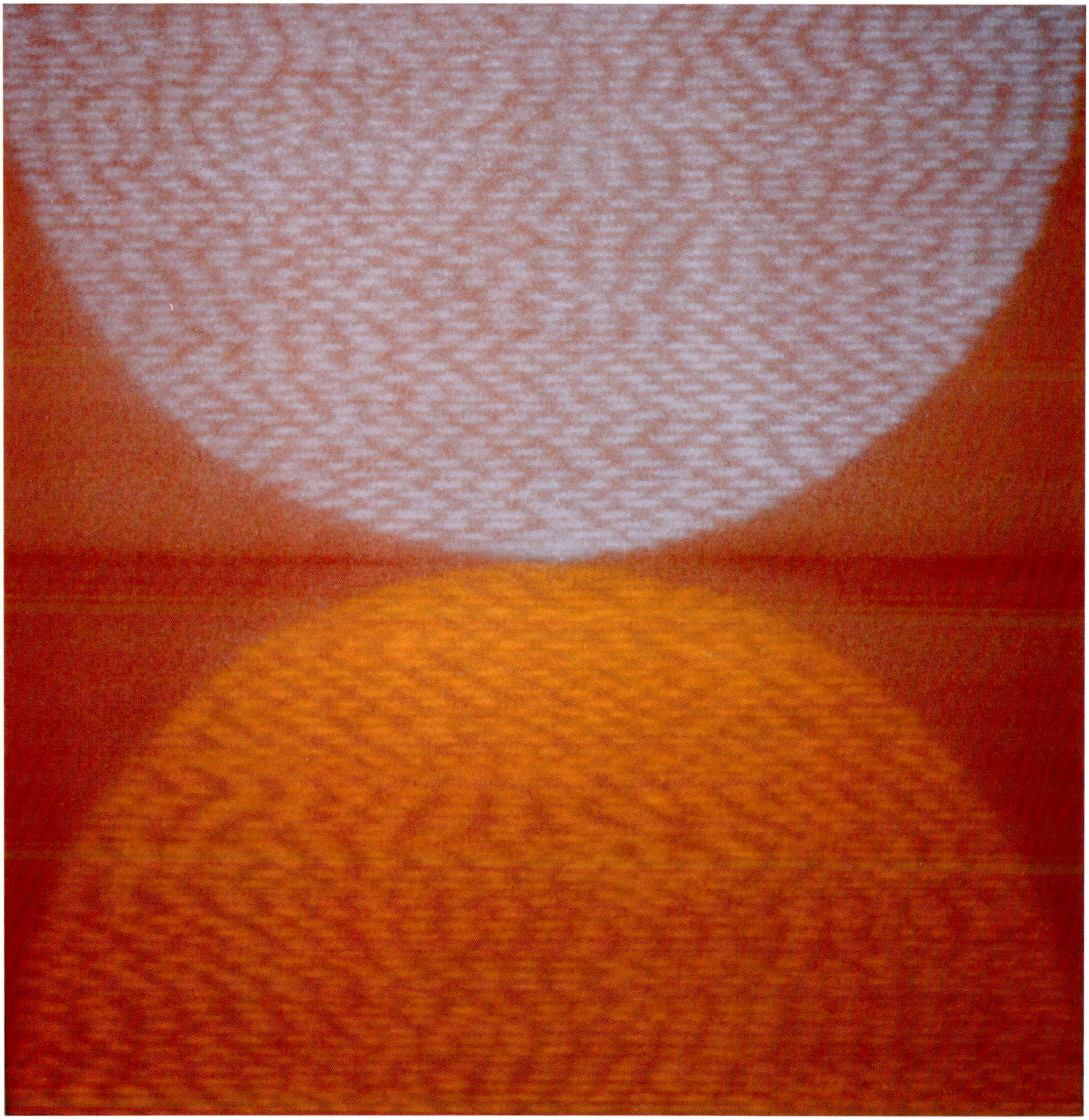

Mirror image
Acrylic & oil on canvas, 91 x 91 cm

The immense weighty orb that bears own in majesty on the naked ball of the galvanized, Seeing Eye. The seeming chaos of the out there world, is to the observant artist, a rigorous order of perfected form, whose image echoes back in grandeur in the deep tinted, open spectral vista down below, as if pressing over, over hanging, so dominating, and yet a self-integrating reality.

Origin
Dry pastels on paper, 25 x 25 cm

Origin
Dry pastels on paper, 25 x 25 cm

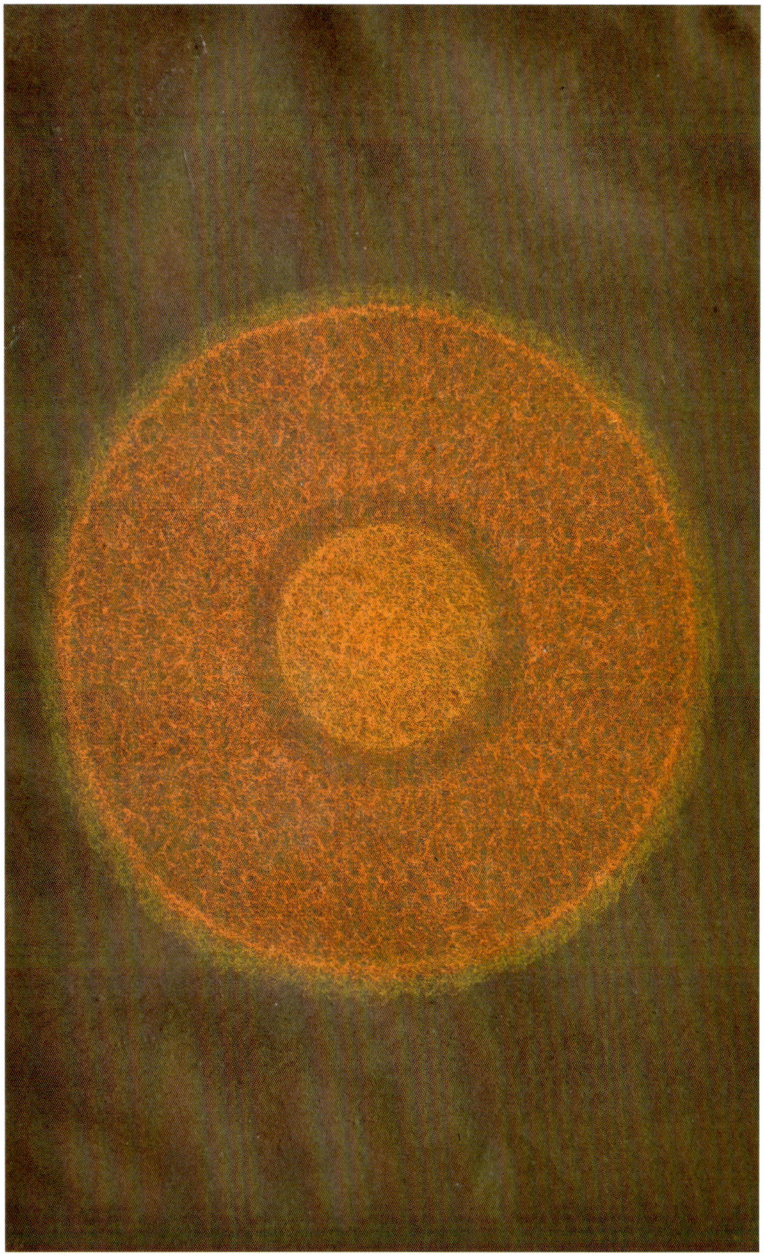

Origin
Dry pastels on canvas, 46 x 28 cm

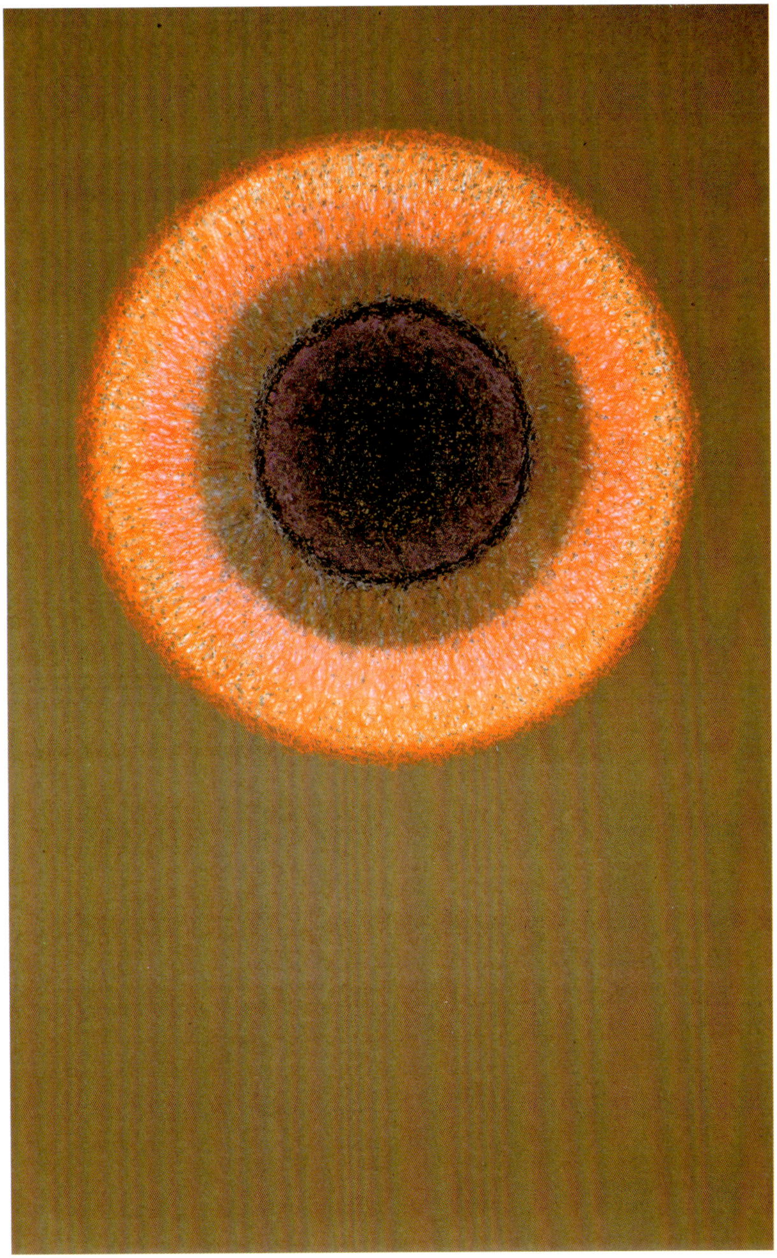

Origin
Dry pastels on canvas, 46 x 28 cm

Lay no finger on it

Music! - - a gross body cast away,
and returning the air of mystery;

No thing announced, only pure being - -
the one supremely itself;

Sounding by electric poles
in far lone fields, the vacant lots;

Heard in all zones,
on five continents;

In jets flying high
above the clouds' foam-cushion,

On racing cars, speeding trains - -
its magic touching wing and wheel;

By words ungraspable, it still hovers here,
in the abstracted mind;

Lay no finger on it - -
it, that finger will not find.

Keshav Malik

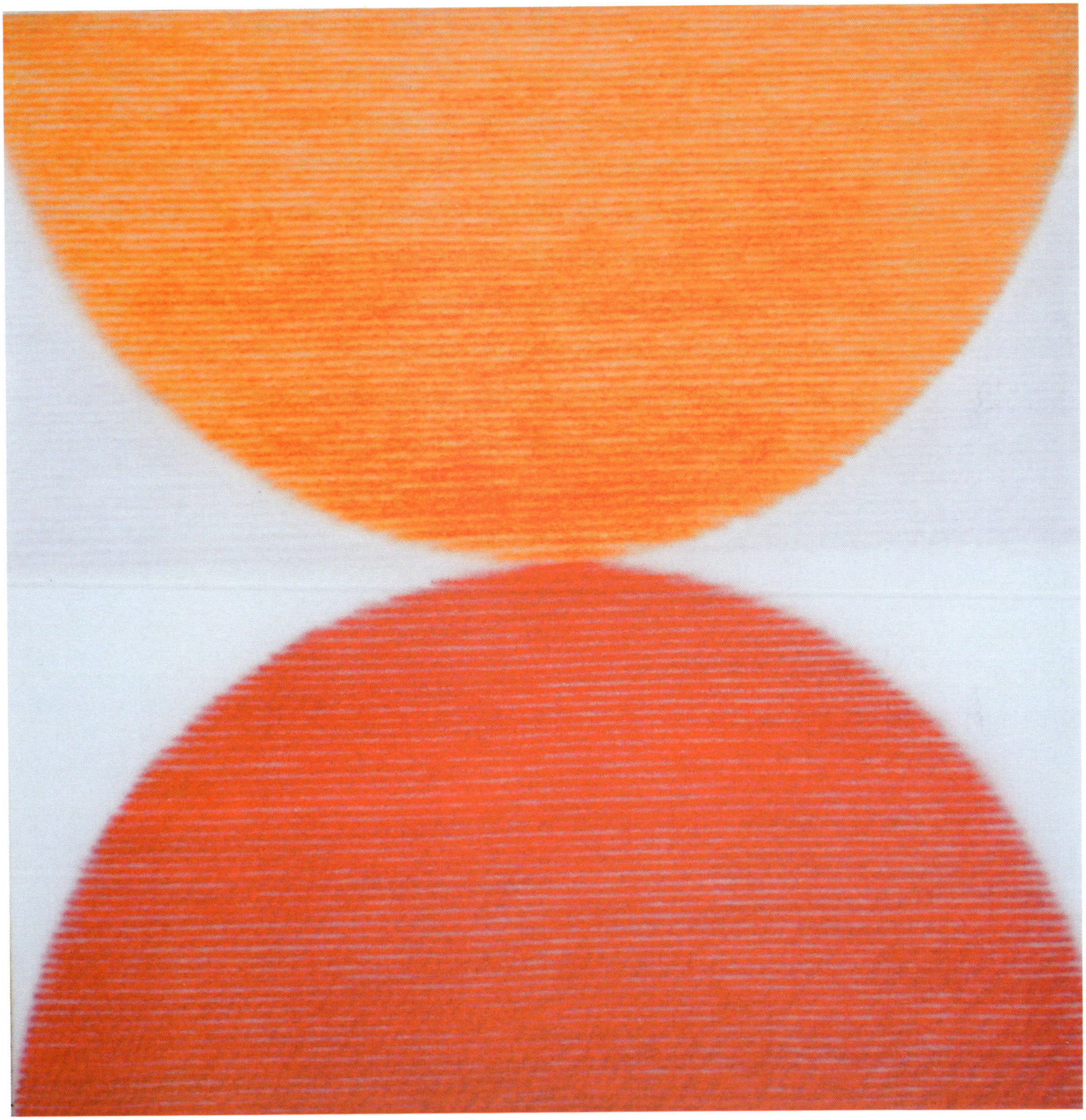

Reflection
Acrylic & oil on canvas, 91 x 91 cm

Origin
Dry pastels on paper, 25 x 25 cm

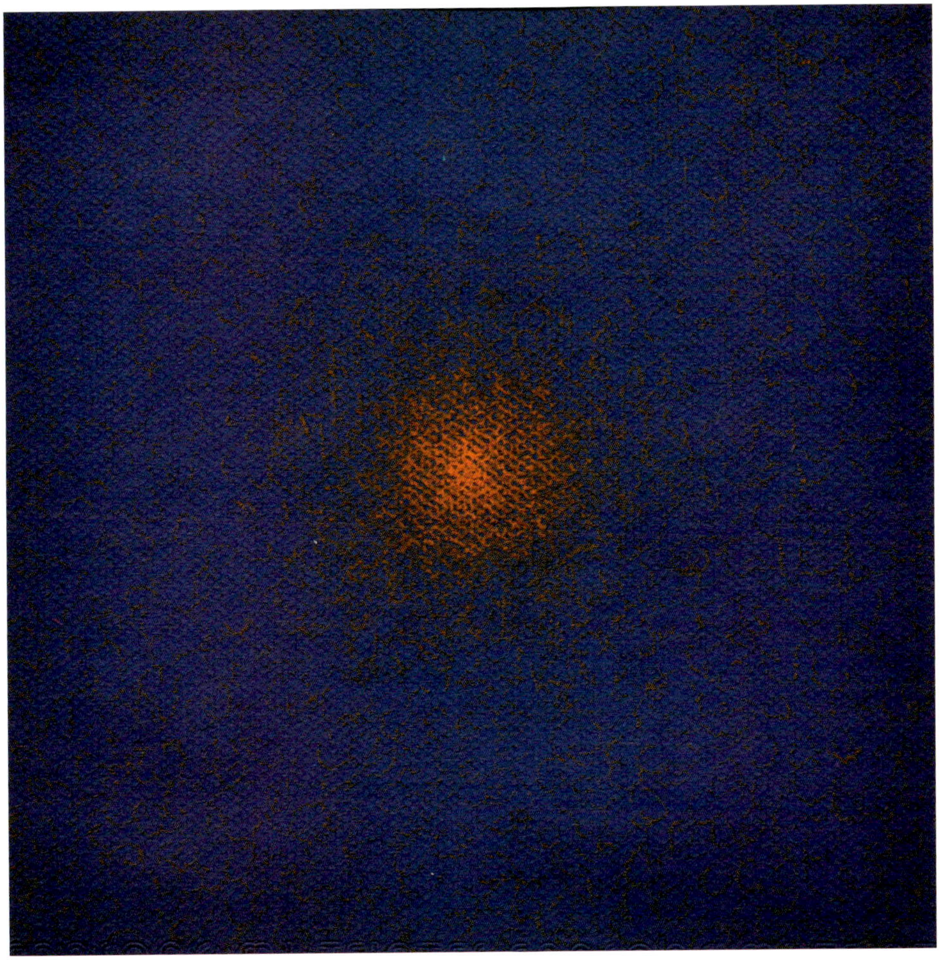

Origin
Dry pastels on paper, 25 x 25 cm

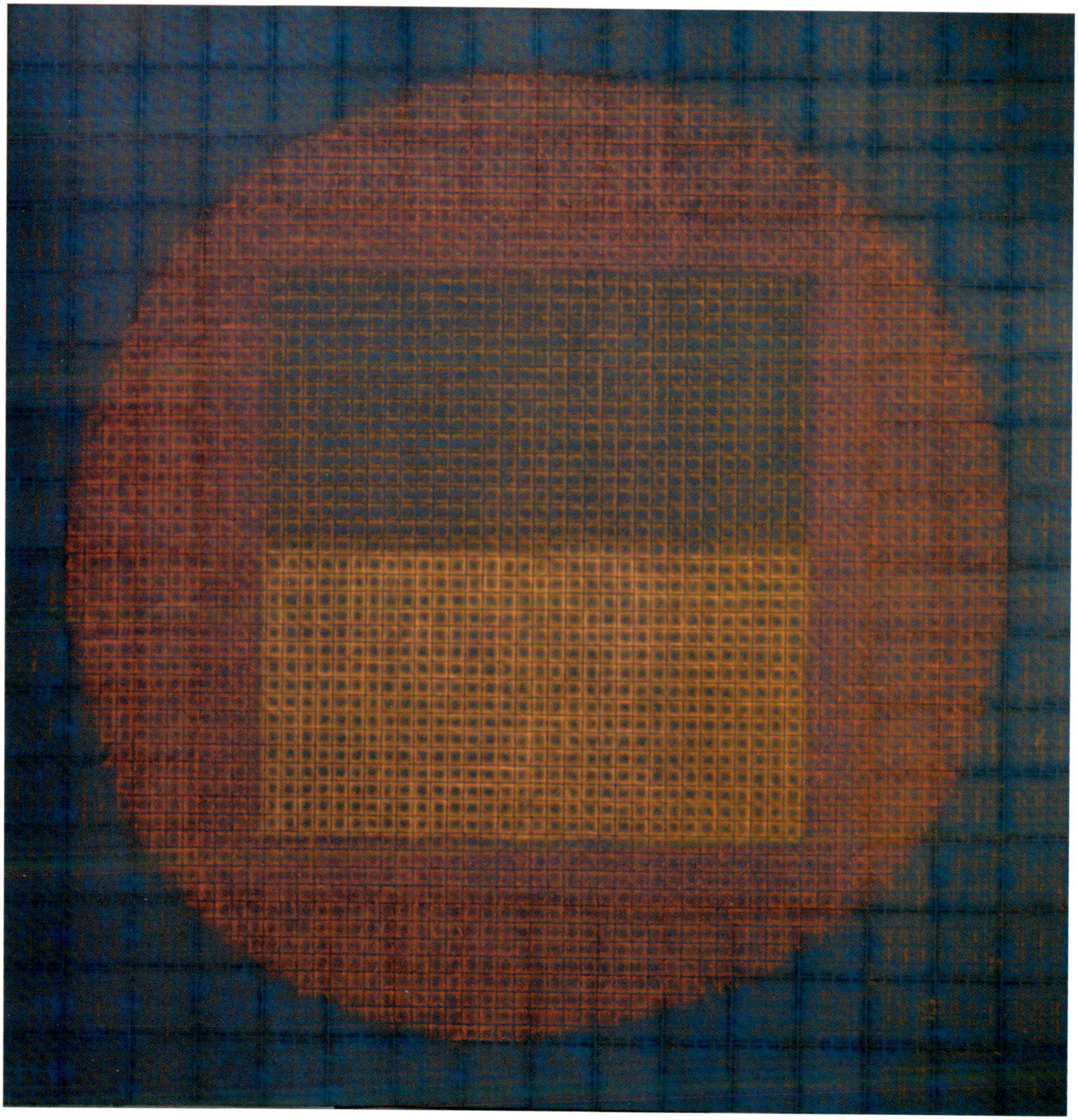

Untitled
Oil on canvas, 122 x 122 cm

This deeply pigmented work stimulates a veiled, behind the appearances, truth, as it were. A message that comes to us obliquely, of a tablet with its age-old mystery and which, surely in turn announces the eternity of the ever revolving astral spheres.

What the artist does in this work, as often in similar media, is seen doing is to get at the grand, seemingly whirling total of immense space with its infinite scintillating dance in concentric circles, of bright particles, and which still awes and amazes the earthlings, no matter all his scientific guess work, all his know-how.

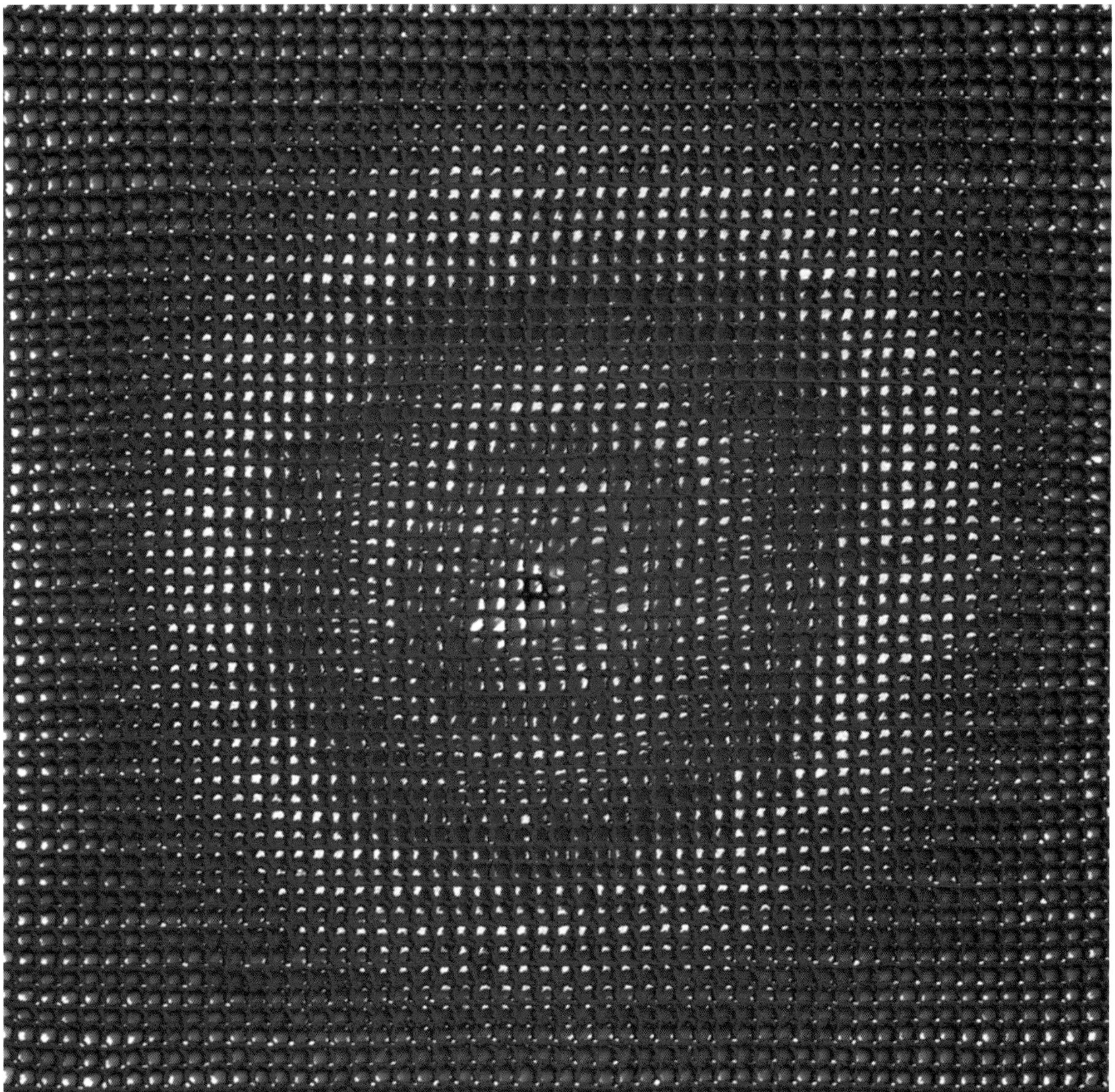

Cosmic dance
Wool on canvas, 76 x 76 cm

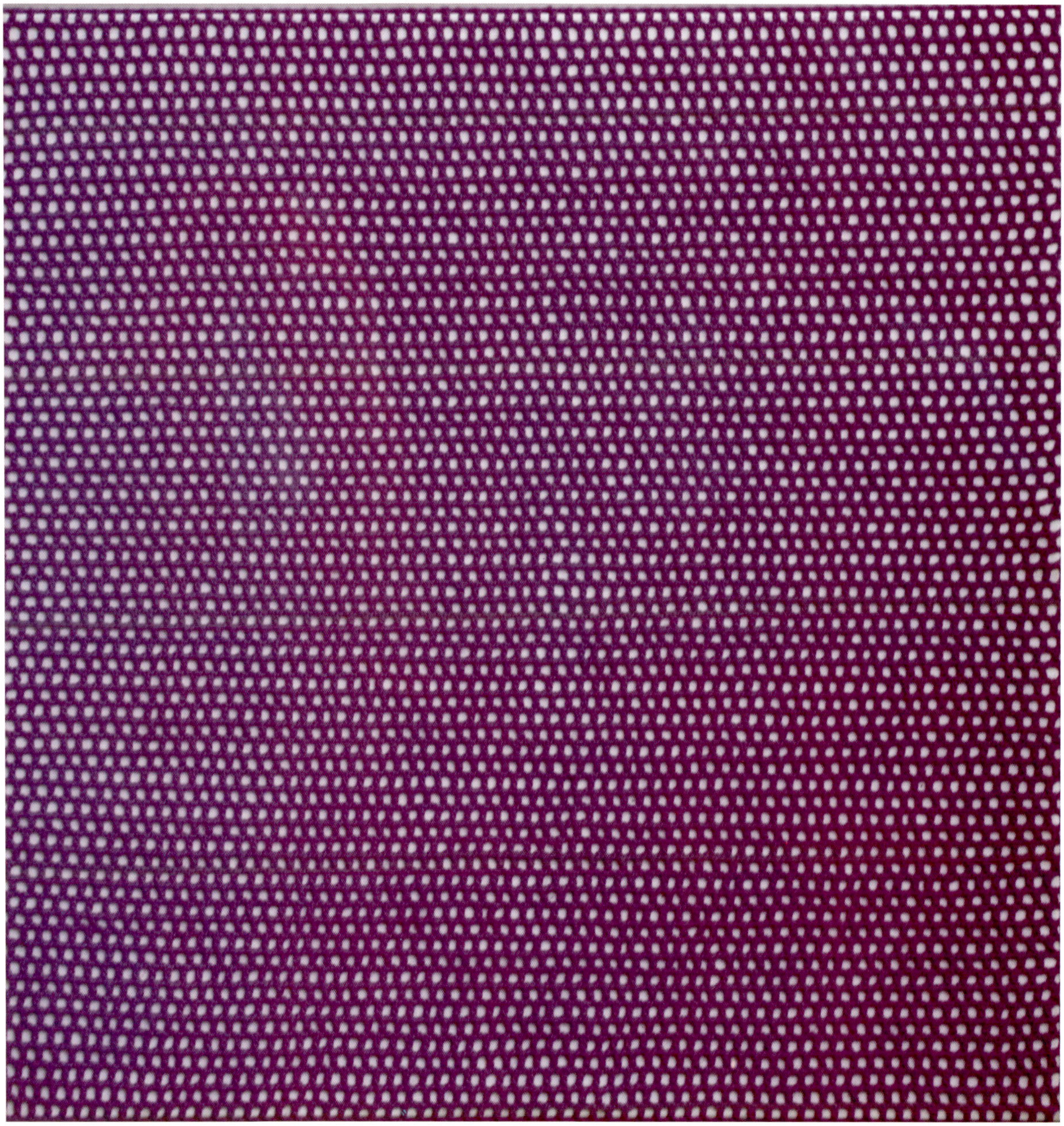

Untitled
Wool on canvas, 76 x 76 cm

With this composition we have a pointillist piano play of events in time-----those never ending happenings that suggest the scenario, the stage-set, of time into space in eternal sequential continuity, of a seamless unity.

Origin
Dry pastels on paper, 25 x 25 cm

Origin
Dry pastels on paper, 25 x 25 cm

Here is the fine-spun web of the architecture of reality. In it the analytic, almost microscopic eye, is brought out in relief.
A sampling of the face of the universe in its rigorous order.

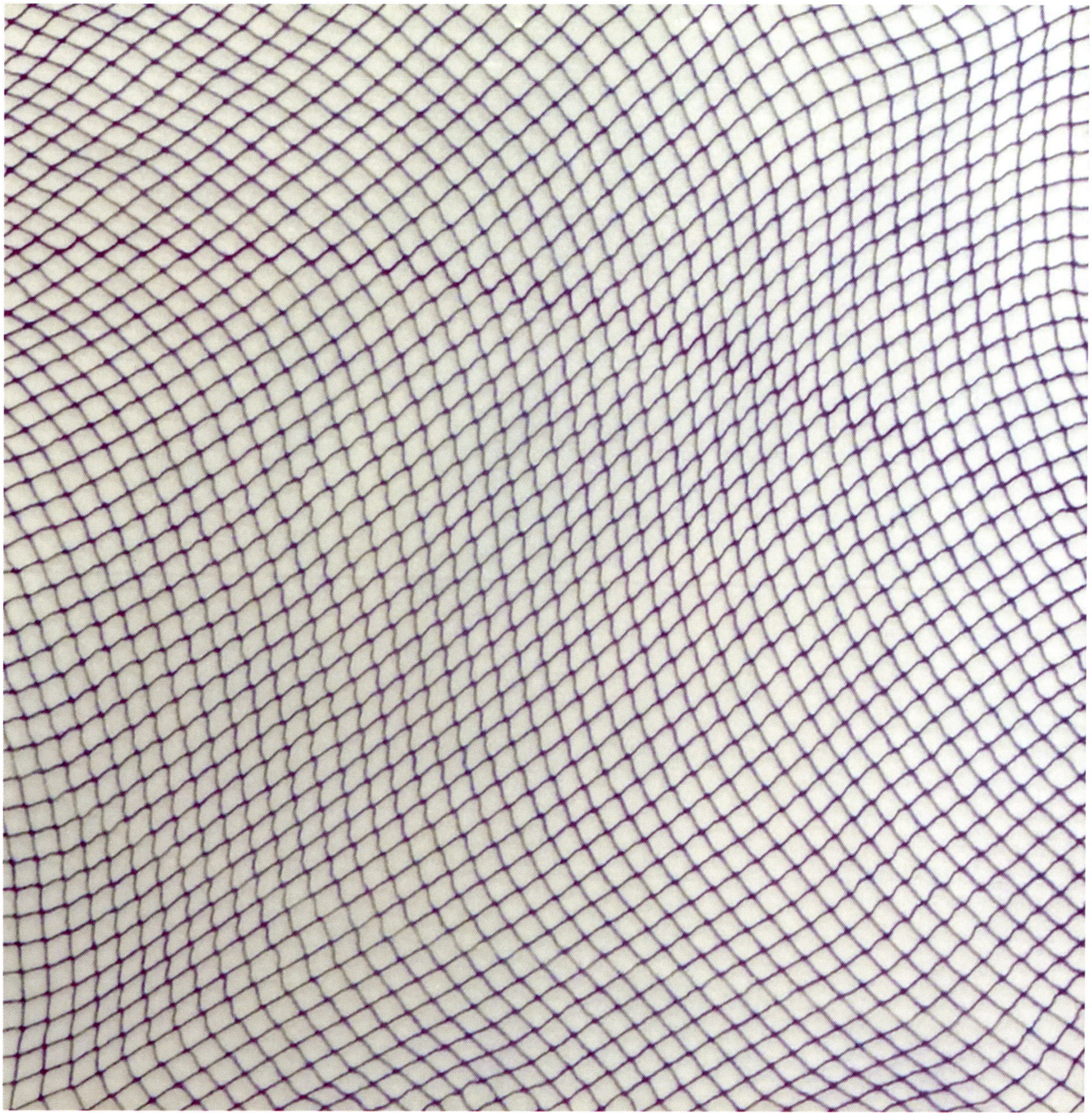

Untitled
Thread on canvas, 61 x 61 cm

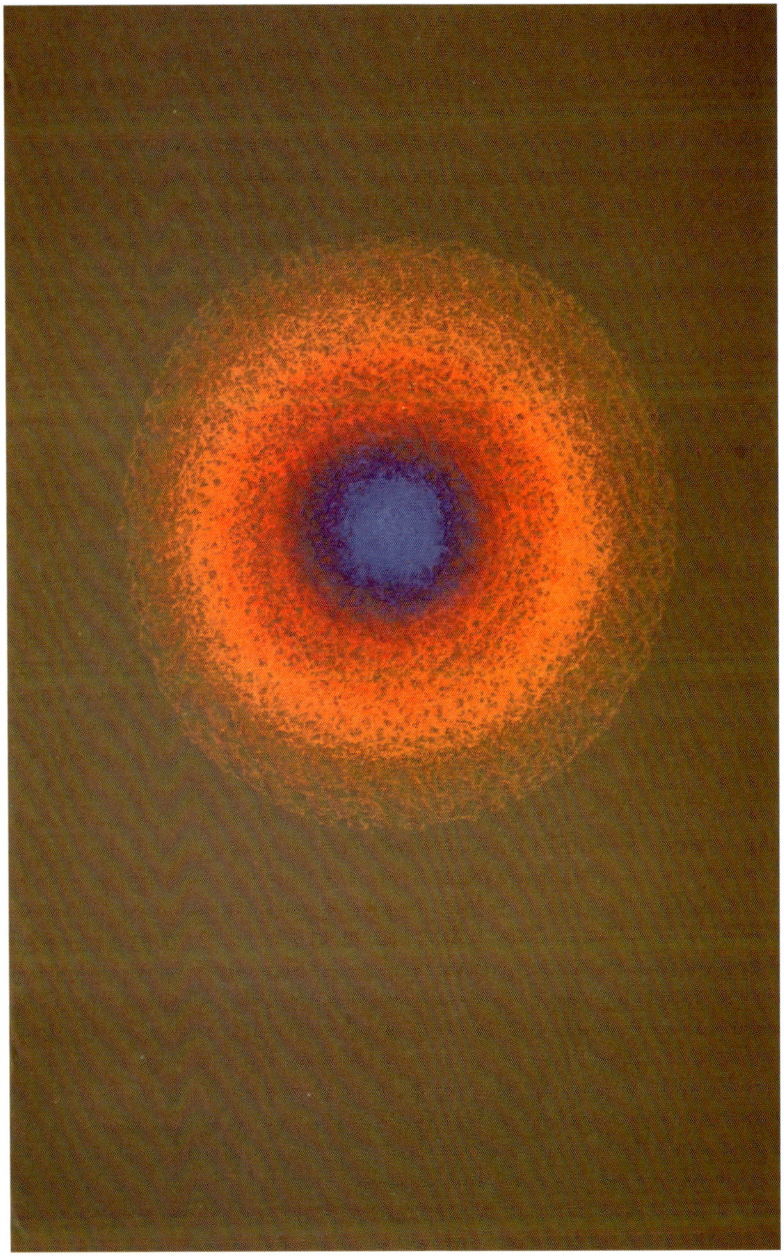

Origin
Dry pastels on canvas, 46 x 28 cm

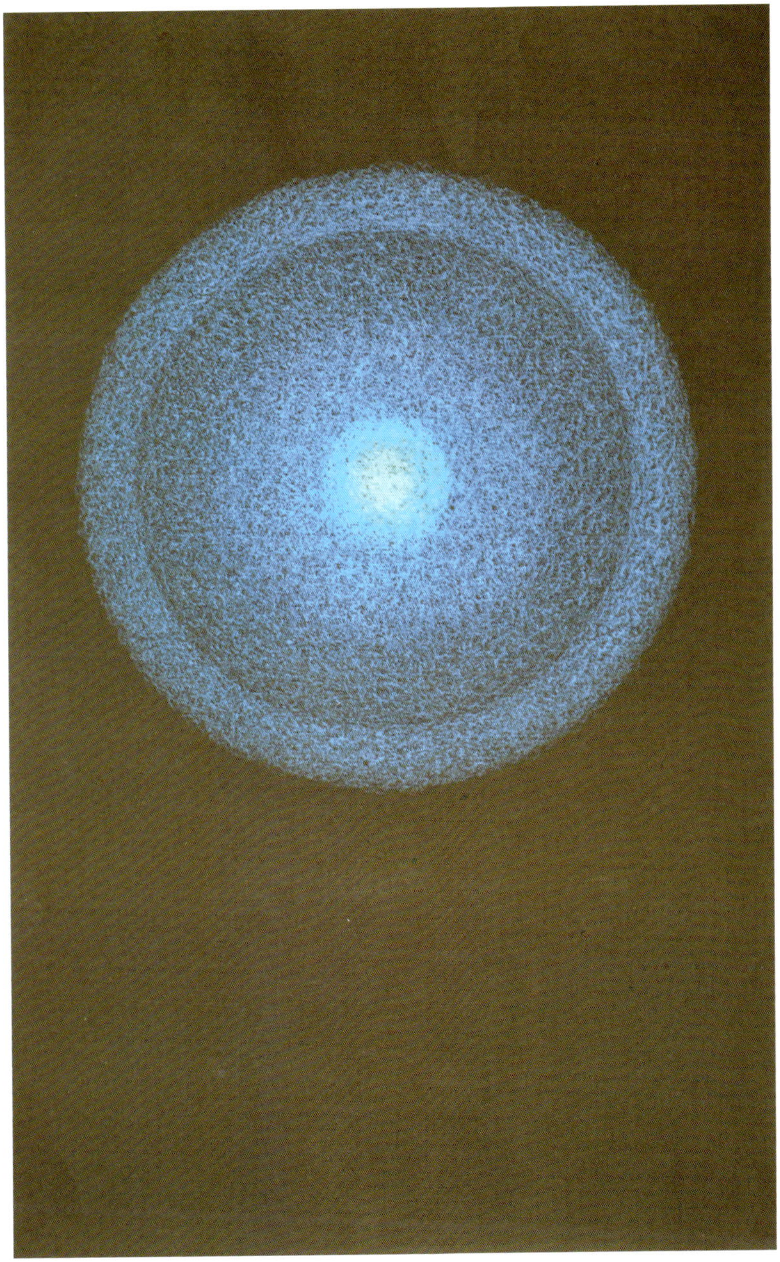

Origin
Dry pastels on canvas, 46 x 28 cm

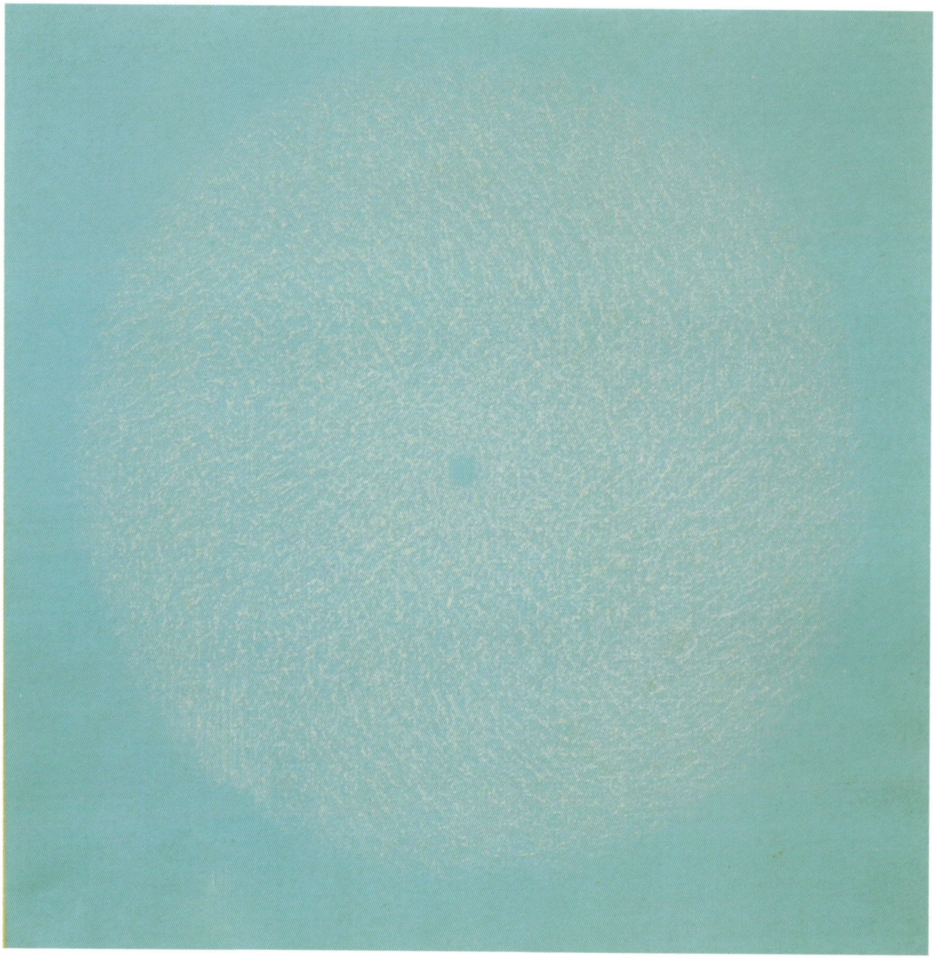

Origin
Dry pastels on paper, 25 x 25 cm

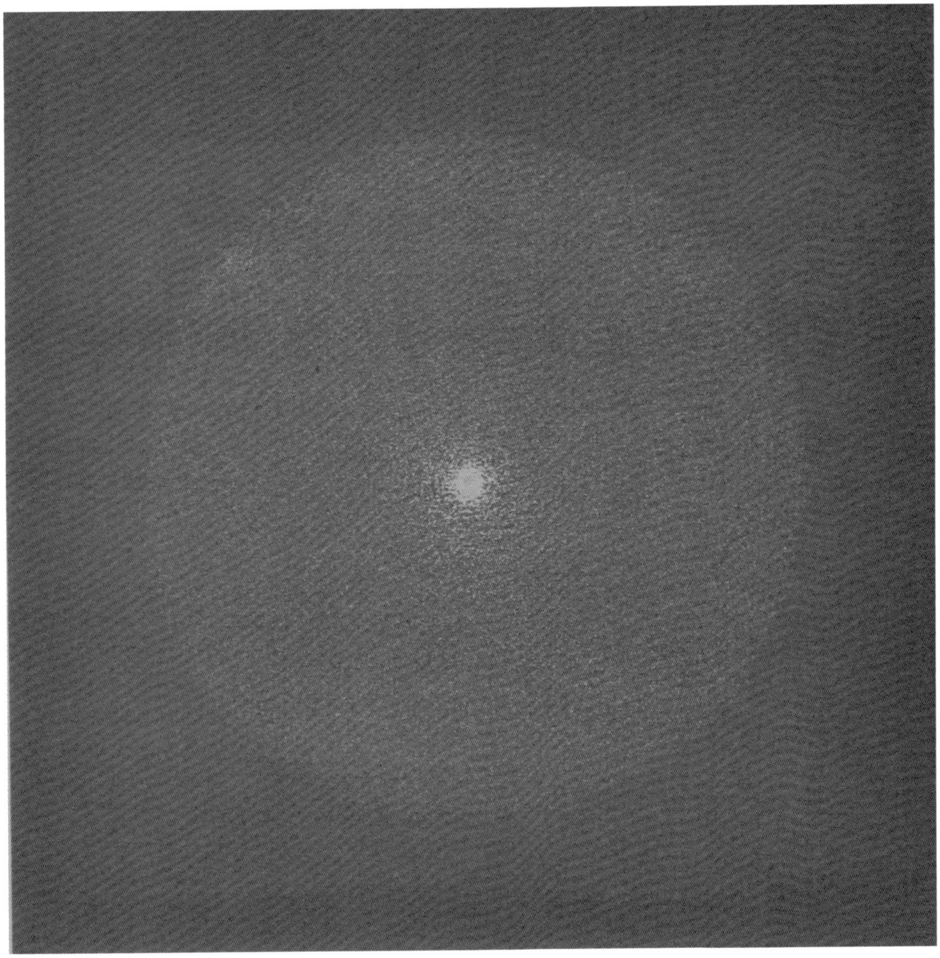

Origin
Dry pastels on paper, 25 x 25 cm

Untitled
Wool on canvas, 91 x 91 cm

Leave Taking

Now bye bye muse - -
eyes by sea-mist dimmed,
I plunge into depths
greater than your own.

Slow but steady I sink
to rock bottoms, though where - -
in water like blue-black ink - -
the head-light is a bright-star.

There heard, of soft sobbing, no sound - -
as by the world's wailing-walls,
no wringing of calloused hands
before solid steel bars.

Muse, from your tearful scene I depart
retreat to a circle of perfect repose - -
drawing close
to the planet's mythic, magnetic floor.

Muse, eyes by sea-mist dimmed;
a row of shiny arrows guides
my smooth decline
to the great quiet.

Keshav Malik

Origin
Dry pastels on paper, 25 x 25 cm

Origin
Dry pastels on paper, 25 x 25 cm

In Transition

Once more tonight
the circling earth is circling
the itself circling sun.
Murmuring but murmuring
do its tides turn from side to side,
till the spat out froth does,
to a complete wash white,
an ocean very very dark and wide.
Observing with deep intent,
the sluggish blood in your own veins
to a pitch ascends - -
going straight to your head.
And then, some more the unbelievable visions,
whole worlds seen in transition.

Keshav Malik

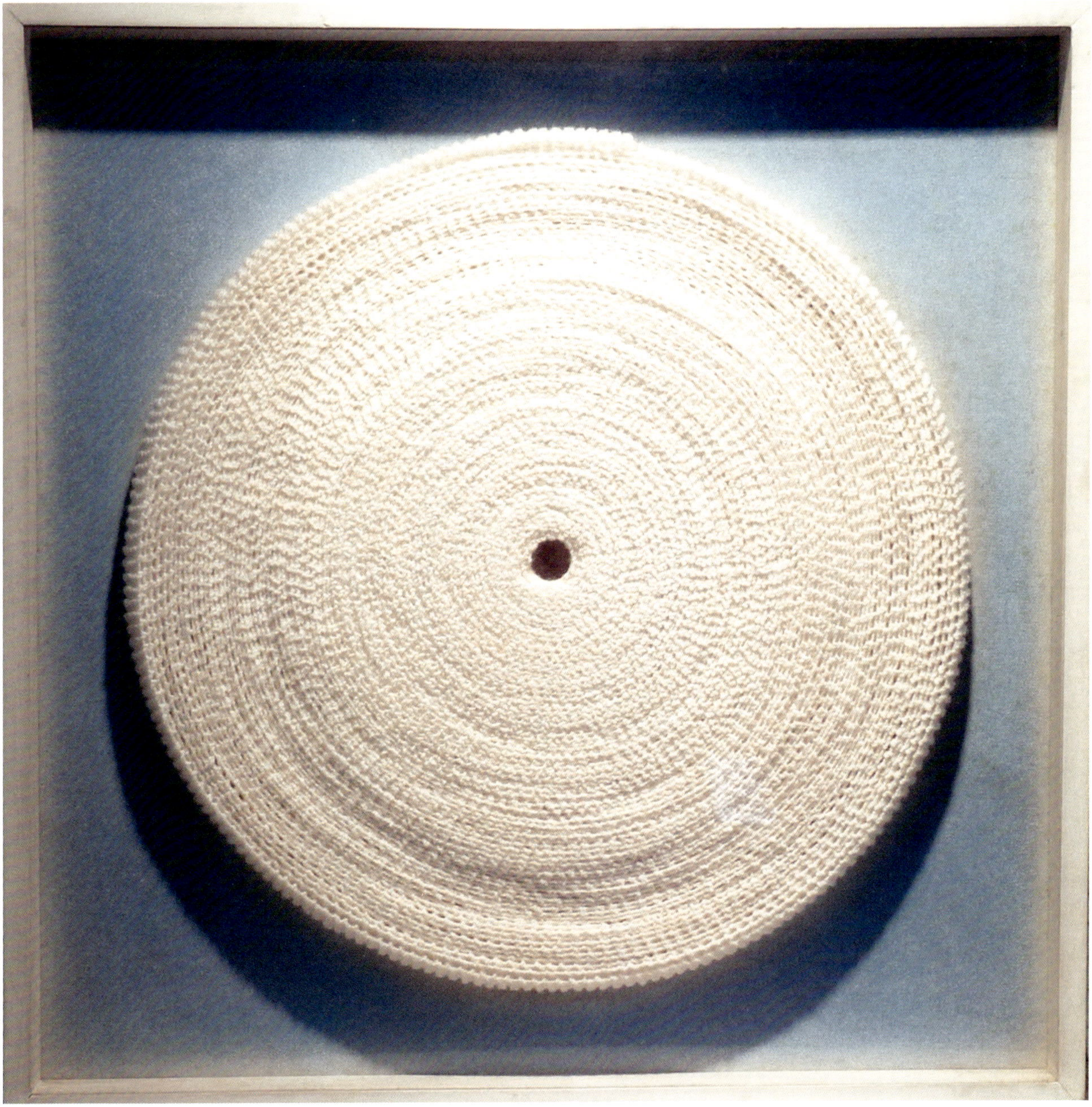

Vesture of Being
Knitted wool on canvas, 61 x 61 cm

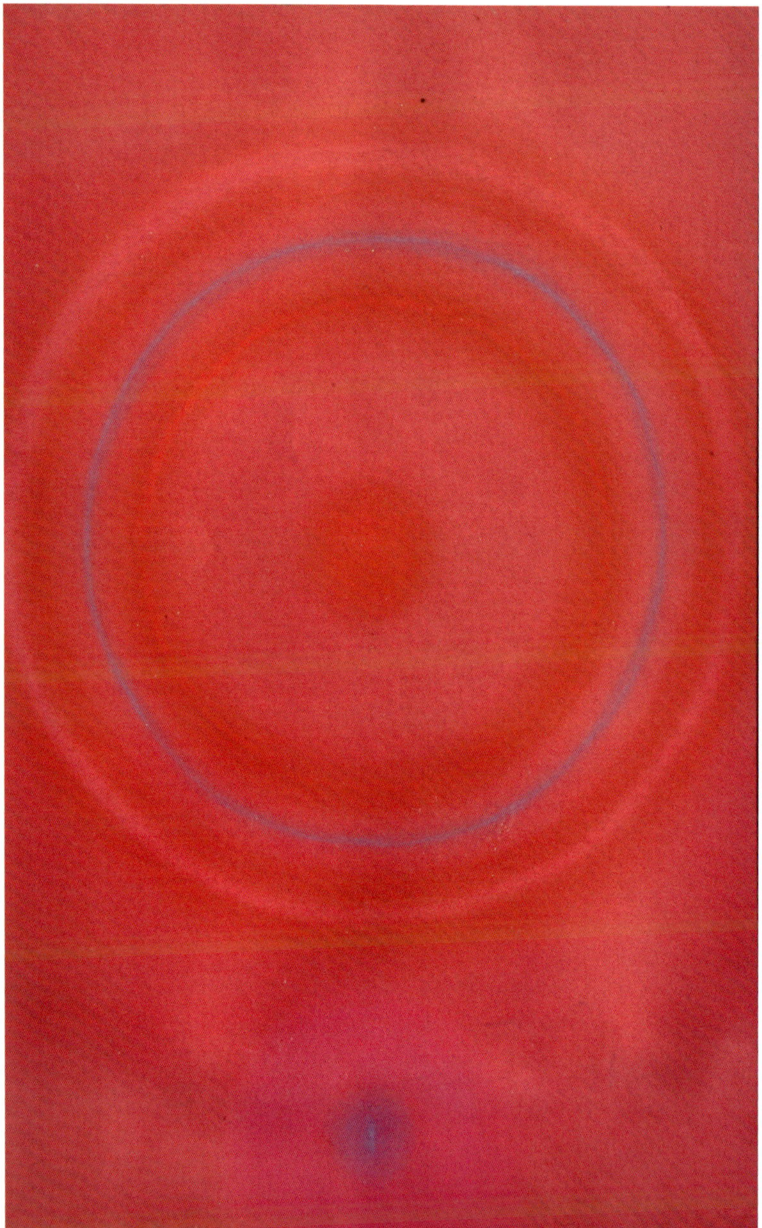

Origin
Dry pastels on canvas, 46 x 28 cm

In the dim light before one dawn

I saw an apparition nigh
in the dim light before one dawn;
saw a shape, dark, somehow like the letter X,
tower high up in the air.

Who was it there stood thus
astride a man-sized earth- - who?
Siva! was it, Shakti!- - or what other
great god or goddess of yore?

I could not tell, I could not,
and yet knelt down low
beneath this so overmastering a force
on bended knee like a z - -

A knight commanded
before a faceless Sire.

Keshav Malik

SHOBHA BROOTA

b. 1943 Delhi, India.

1964 Diploma in Fine Arts, College of Art, Delhi.

1962 Sangeet Visharad, Masters in vocal Indian classical Music.

AWARDS

1982 AIFACS

1986 Sahitya Kala Parishad, Delhi.

1982-84 Scholarship, Ministry of Culture, Govt of India.

1989-92 Fellowship-Ministry of Culture, Govt. of India (Again in years 1996-98).

SOLO SHOWS

1964-97 Delhi, India.

1985 Aakkar Gallery, Chandigarh.

1992 Schoo's Gallery, Amsterdam; Rebecca Hossack Gallery, London.

1994 Jehangir Art Gallery, Bombay; ABC Gallery, Varanasi; Gallery 42, Delhi.

1997 Retrospective of Prints', Art Konsult, Delhi; Edith Cowen University, Perth.

– International Studio A.F.W.A., Fermantle, Australia.

2003 Music of the Spheres, Visual Art Gallery, New Delhi.

– Birla Academy of Arts & Craft, Kolkata.

2006 Song of the Devine, Pallete Art Gallery, New Delhi.

2007 Edge of Infinity, Indigo Blue Art, Singapore.

2008 A Path Beyond, AICON Gallery, Palo Alto, California.

2013 Vesture of Being, India International Centre, Art Gallery, New Delhi.

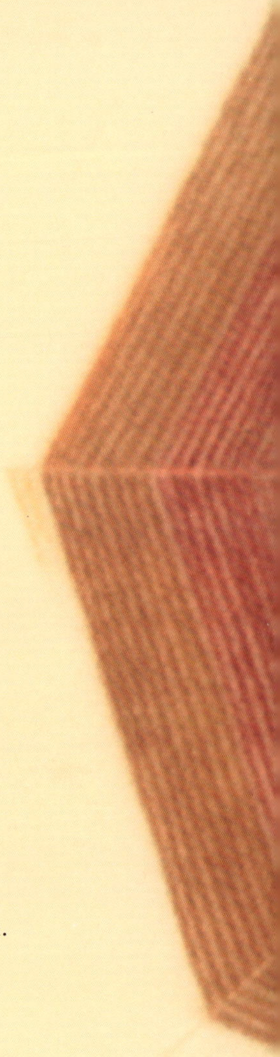

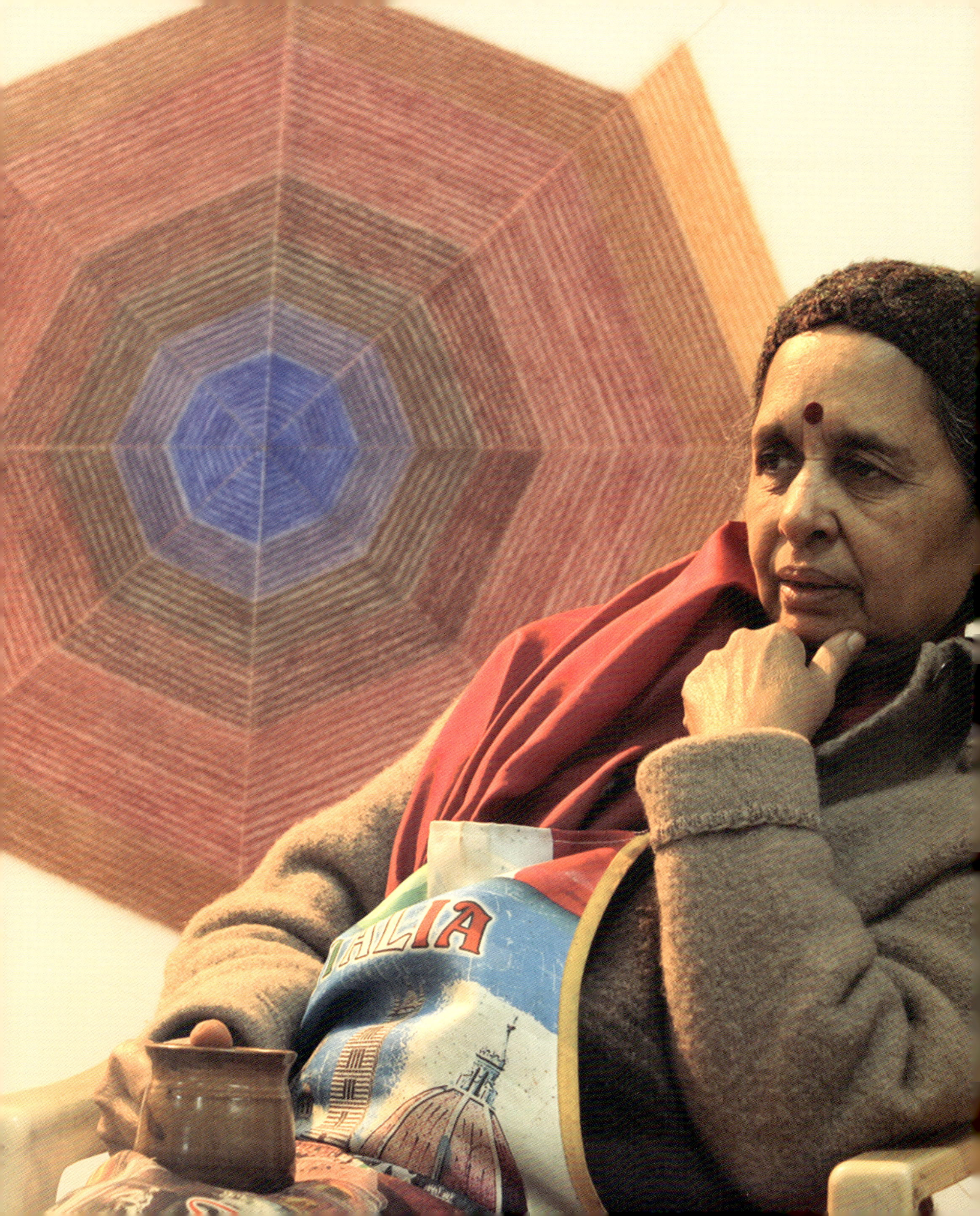
ALIA

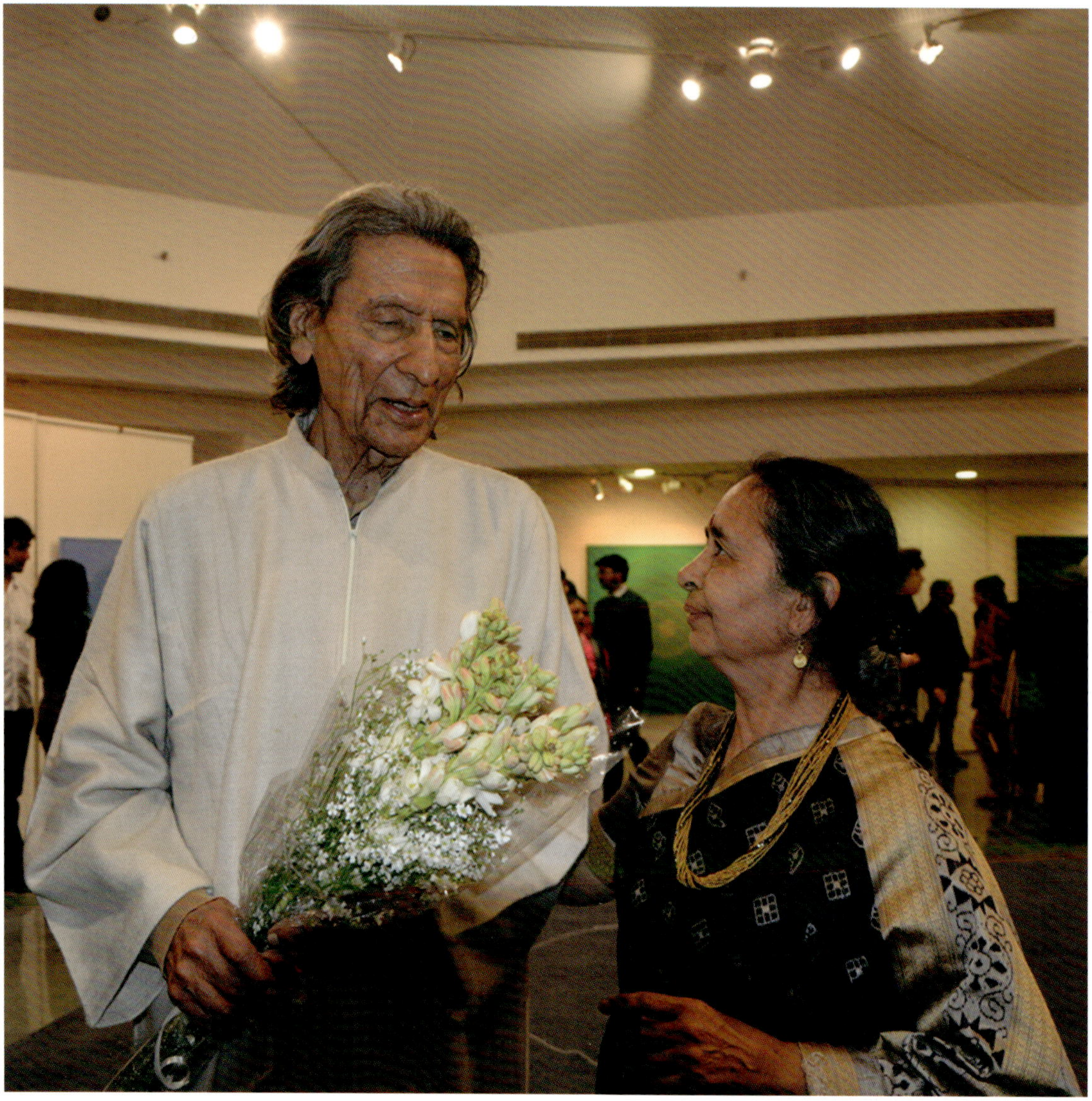

The artist with poet and art critic Keshav Malik.

SELECTED PARTICIPATIONS

1975	International Women Artists, Delhi.
1983	Print Biennial, Bhopal; Art Biennial, Bangladesh.
1984	Exhibition of Contemporary Art, Tokyo.
1986	6th Triennial India, Delhi.
1986-87	Women Artists, NGMA, New Delhi, Bulgaria, Yugoslavia.
1988	Abstract Art, Gallery Art and Data, Frankfurt.
1990	Malaysian Experience / Malaysian Images, Kaula Lumpur.
-	Contemporary Prints, curated by Antonio Muratore, Melbourne.
-	Asian European Art Biennial, Ankara; Ambassador's Choice, NGMA, New Delhi.
1991	9 Contemporary Indian Artists,Gemeetemuseum Arnhem, Netherlands.
-	ILSud Del Mondol, Gallery Civica D' Arte, Marsala, Palermo, Milano, Italy.
-	Soulcatchers, curated by Rebecca Hossack, London.
1992	Art for a Fairer World, by Oxfam, Glasgow, Cardiff, London.
-	Balder Aus Indien, curated by Edda Bhattacharya, Hamburg.
1993	Indische Gegenwarskunst, Mainz, Germany and Stettin, Poland.
-	V. Tudatusaag, Budapest, Hungary.
1994	8th Triennial India, Delhi; Contemporary Miniatures, CIMA, Calcutta.
-	100 years of Indian Art, NGMA, India.
-	40 Indian Artists, Tiazcala, Mexico.
1995	Abstract 95, CIMA, Calcutta.
-	Sothbeys Auction, London.
1997	Chhoo Mantar, Exhibition of Magnetic Art, Art Konsult, New Delhi.
1998	Symbolism and Geometry in Modern Art, NGMA, India.
-	WWF Auction, New Delhi
-	International Artists, IASG (Washington DC), New Delhi
-	Small, James Harvey, Sydney.

–	Indian Artists, Vedanta Gallery, Chicago.
1999	Senior Fellowship Artists, Delhi.
–	Abstract Schematic, curated by Peter Nagy, Nature Morte, New Delhi.
2001	Kaleidoscope, Singapore.
2002-13	India-Korea, New Delhi and Korea-India, Seoul, South Korea.
2003	Solitude, The White Show, curated by Dr. Alka Pande, Visual Art Gallery, New Delhi.
–	Kerela Lalit Kala Akademy Collection Show, Calcutta.
–	Annual Show, of Palette Gallery, New Delhi.
2004	Devotional Breach, curated by Peter Nagy, Sumukha Gallery, Bangalore.
2004-05	Spirit of the Century, Kumar Art Gallery, New Delhi.
2005	Negotiating Matters, curated by Roobina Karode at Anant Art Gallery, New Delhi.
–	Resonance, Fifty Years of Lalit Kala Academy, New Delhi.
–	Roop Vidhan, Expression of Abstract, Art Alive, New Delhi.
2006	Eleventh Harmony Art Show, Mumbai.
2007	25 Contemporary Indian Artists, organized by Nicolas Vourriaud and Ravi Kumar, Moscow and other places in Russia and also in Paris.
–	Indian Color, curated by Euri Seong at Keumsan Gallery, Seoul, Korea, organized by Peter Nagy of Nature Morte and Vadehara Galleries of New Delhi.
–	Surfaces and Textures, organized by Gallery Espace, Delhi and Ganges Art, Kolkata, at Ganges Art, Kolkata.
–	Diverse Voices, Galleria, Hongkong; Sothbeys auction, New York.
–	Conglomeration, Indian Contemporary Artists, by Prakrit Arts, Mumbai.
–	Annual Show of Palette Gallery, New Delhi.
2008	Contradictions and Complexities: Contemporary Art from India, curated by Patricia Hamilton and Peter Nagy, Western Project, Los Angeles, USA.
–	Dus Mahavidyas, ten creative forces – a book conceived and curated by Ravi Kumar, shows in New Delhi, Banglore and Mumbai.

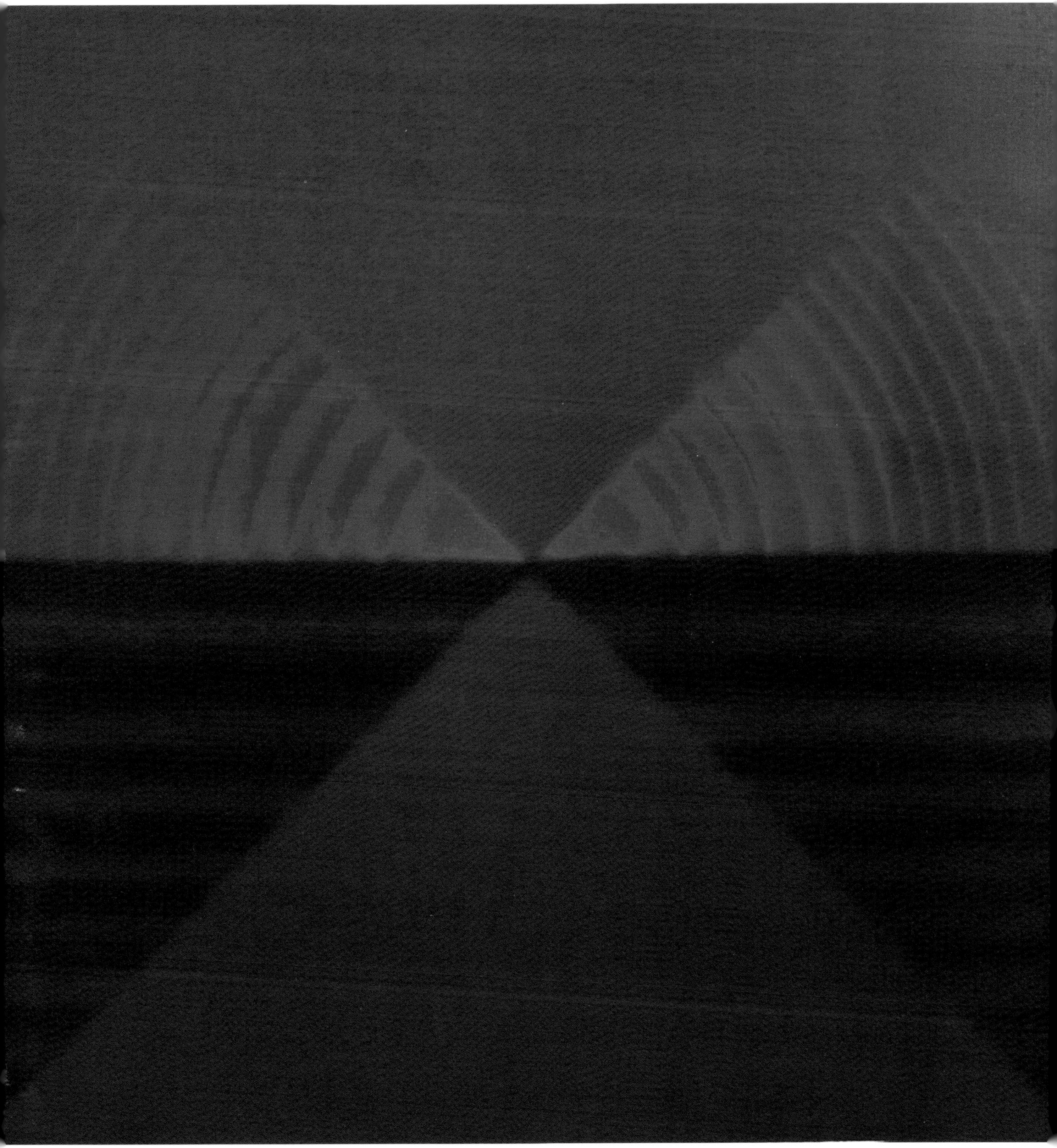

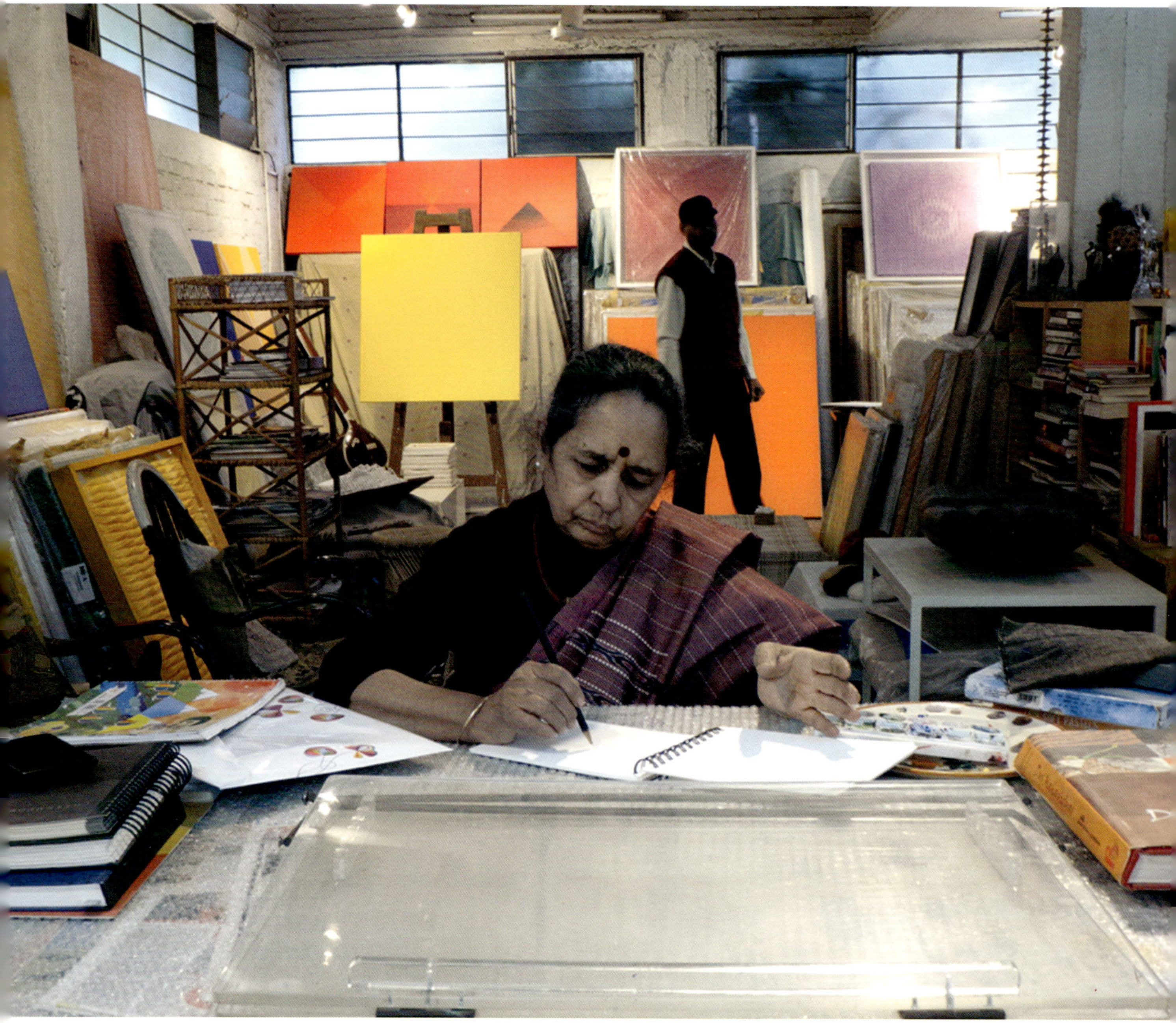

-	Frame Figure Field, Delhi Art Gallery, New Delhi.
2009	Menifestation IV, Delhi Art Gallery, New Delhi.
2010	Devotion-Transformation, curated by Sushma K. Bahl, Art Positive Gallery, New Delhi.
-	Between Ambivalence and Criticism, contemporary abstraction, Art Konsult Gallery, New Delhi.
2011	Visual Ventures, by Emami Chisel Gallery, Kolkata.
-	Roots—Routes, by Gallery Ganesha, New Delhi.
-	Devotion, by Art Positive Gallery, New Delhi.
-	Feminnale, by Grill and Lounge, New Delhi.
2012	Ebony And Ivory, by Gallery Art Perspective, New Delhi.
-	Recent Works by 33 Modern And Contemporary Indian Artists, by Suryaveer Kohli Art, New Delhi.
-	China India Imaginings and Transformations, Macquarie University Art gallery, Sydney, Australia.
-	SNO 89, Contemporary Art Project, Sydney, Australia.
2013	Art Fair 2013, by Gallery Art Positive, New Delhi.

INVITATIONS

1990	Artist in Residency, National Gallery, Kaula Lumpur.
1997	Artist in Residency Edith Cowen University, Perth, W. Australia.
-	Artist in Residency, Artist foundation of W. Australia, Fremantle.
2005	Invited by Guyana Govt. to paint the portrait of Dr. Chaddi Jagan, Ex. President of Guyana, for their Parliament House.

COLLECTIONS

Works in numerous collections such as National Gallery in India and Malaysia.

Private collections of E. M. Schoo, Chester Herwitz and many others in India and abroad.

Studio and residence in New Delhi, India. Contact: *shobhabroota@gmail.com*